AN INTRODUCTION TO FORENSIC ANTHROPOLOGY

By

SURINDER NATH

WITH A FOREWORD BY

V.N. SEHGAL

DIRECTOR

CENTRAL FORENSIC SCIENCE LABORATORY

NEW DELHI

GYAN

ISBN : 978-81-212-0242-8

Published, 2018

Published by

Gyan Publishing House
5, Ansari Road
Daryaganj, New Delhi-110002
Phone: 011-47034999, 9811692060
www.gyanbooks.com
E-mail: books@gyanbooks.com

Printed at: G. Print Process, Delhi.

FOREWORD

Kudos to Dr. Surinder Nath for writing an excellent book on Forensic Anthropology. It is a welcome addition to the books and articles on this discipline, since for the last many years the need for an introductory text and reference was strongly felt by the specialists as well as the amateurs. Eminently qualified to fulfil this task, Dr. Nath, with a commanding lucidity of language has accomplished this work which optimally treats these aspects of forensic anthropology, which hitherto were not adequately dealt with even in books generally quoted as reference books by judiciary.

It is not only that he has eruditely taken care of all the recent works in forensic anthropology and its cognate disciplines, but also has assimilated all this with his experience of teaching and research in this discipline for the last thirteen years.

For a long time, forensic anthropology did not have a distinct place but was nurtured in the womb of physical anthropology, and it was classed along with other sections of applied physical anthropology. Its adjunct status is no more acceptable as 'anthropology applied for forensic purposes' is now 'forensic anthropology', with an identity of its own. Now forensic anthropology is a *sine qua non* for a scientific investigation of crimes. Dr. Nath abundantly shows that techniques and methods which have been the prerogatives of ethno-archaeology, palaeontology, human biology and population genetics have been coherently integrated in the perspectives of forensic anthropology. Any one interested in forensic science, medical jurisprudence, medico-legal investigations and criminology will be immensely benefited by his work.

I again congratulate Dr. Nath for this pithy work on forensic anthropology. I am elated to write that this work is indispensable for both the scientists and people engaged in field and on-the-spot investigations. Moreover, for judicial purposes wherever evidence on skeletonised material is involved, Dr. Nath's book will be an authoritative reference and thus it will serve both the investigating police officers and court in a fruitful manner for administering justice.

Director
Central Forensic Science
Laboratory (C.B.I.)
New Delhi.

V.N. SEHGAL

PREFACE

I have been associated with the programme of teaching forensic science and forensic anthropology in the University of Delhi for the last thirteen years. In the curriculum of post-graduate course in anthropology, forensic anthropology occupies an important place and a branch which was earlier a part of applied physical anthropology, has now not only achieved differentiation, but has emerged as a distinct discipline. Besides contributing towards the theoretical aspects of anthropology, forensic anthropology is indispensable to crime investigation. In the course of its growth, it has developed its own battery of techniques, analytical propositions, and research potential. Drawing mainly from the repertoire of anthropological works, forensic anthropology interacts with other disciplines oriented towards an understanding of crime and its investigation, like criminology, medical jurisprudence, and forensic medicine.

In spite of these developments—applied as well as theoretical—which are clearly stated by the number of publications and research projects, the discipline of forensic anthropology has always been lacking an introductory book which collates together the meaning and scope of the subject that has been lying dispersed in several general and specialized publications. Often for introducing the subject to the beginners in forensic anthropology, we have been relying on scanty material in books published from the developed countries. These books do succeed in giving an outline of the discipline, but fail to put all the aspects together. And moreover, since these books are written in contexts different from ours, most of their examples and quantifications do not suit the Indian material. Unfortunately these books do not reach the Indian market and even if few do they are out of reach of average Indian students and the practitioners. Therefore there has been a pressing need of an introductory book in forensic anthropology, which not only weaves all the achievements of the discipline together, but takes an astute cognizance of the Indian situation and material. This book is a humble attempt in that direction.

Forensic anthropology can be defined as that branch of physical anthropology which for forensic purposes deals with the identification of more or less skeletonised remains known to be, or at least suspected of being, human. The identification process provides opinions on the sex, age, ethnic group, stature and other characteristics of the individual whose remains are excavated, which may lead to his or her recognition. Identification of an individual is primarily dependent on the morphological features, recognisable through soft parts, and only secondarily, identification takes help of skeletal parts. In cases where soft parts have putrefied beyond recognition, and the coroners fail to render any valuable help, the onus of identification falls only on the skeletonised remains, and the construction of individual identity on them. And in the latter work, the discipline of forensic anthropology extends an inalienable help. Moreover, forensic anthropology has gained a lot from diverse specialisation of anthropology like ethnoarchaeology, palaeoanthropology and human population biology. The techniques and modes of analysis acquired thereby can be used fruitfully for not only drawing inferences from the given skeletonised material but also for in *situ* examination of the remains. Being an applied branch of physical anthropology, its usefulness in crime and medico-legal investigation is greatly acknowledged.

This modest attempt towards introducing the panorama of forensic anthropology has the following layout, and its thumbnail sketch is presented here. This book begins with the subject matter of forensic anthropology and its succinct history.

After stating that material for forensic purposes is the outcome of the natural process of death—natural, accidental, or intentional—there is an examination of death, its types and the process, and the meaning of death in forensic anthropology. This portion besides substantiating the famous statement that 'we die in bits and pieces' goes on towards discussing the questions that arise in the examination of skeletonised material. Questions like, whether the bones belong to human beings ; are they of one individual ; what could be the sex of the individual or individuals ; how tall was the individual ; what could be the age ; to which ethnic stock did the individual belong to ; what could be the cause and time of death ; are there any distinguishing criteria that lead to personal identification, are discussed.

A delineation of the questions that are pertinent to a forensic anthropologist is followed by a detailed account of sex identification from various bones. Besides describing the cranial and pelvic criteria, the post-cranial bones used for sex determination have been discussed. This portion on sex identification is succeeded by a section on the estimation of age. The latter deals with the estimation of age during different developmental stages. Here sex differences in age determination are also noted. A description of primary and secondary ossification centres is followed by a portion on dental germs and estimation of age through them. After detailing out two important variables, sex and age, the book describes the racial differences that can be achieved on the basis of cranial traits.

In the section devoted to reconstruction of stature from skeletal remains, anatomical and mathematical methods for reconstruction of stature have been enunciated. Various regression equations formulated by different authors are listed here. After this, procedures related to reconstruction of stature from bone fragments have been laid out. Moving from stature estimation, the book has two portions, viz., assessment of time and cause of death, and reconstruction of the face, where the forensic anthropologist works in collaboration with medical professionals and prepares the case. In this book procedures regarding the treatment and preservation of skeletal material have also been given.

During the course of most trials, the forensic anthropologist is usually called for giving his or her expert testimony. The section on expert witness and testimony sums up the role and moral ethic of a forensic anthropologist. He or she should remain objective without being influenced by any factor, primordial or otherwise. Thus the book takes the reader from the subject matter of forensic anthropology, to the nuances of forensic work, to finally the role, expectations and moral obligation of its disciplinarians.

I sincerely hope that this effort will serve the needs of the students, researchers and teachers engaged in forensic anthropology and its allied disciplines. Any suggestions for its improvement will be highly appreciated.

SURINDER NATH

ACKNOWLEDGEMENTS

This book is a modest outcome of my activities in the discipline of forensic anthropology. Although the material encompassed in this endeavour is available in scattered form in many books and journals, the whole lot, treated comprehensively and judiciously, is not embodied in a single source. The students as well as the researchers have always hoped for a book introducing them to the discipline and nuances of forensic anthropology. Having been associated with this discipline for more than a decade, I have tried to offer an introductory book which not only brings together almost all the existing material, but also provides a holistic statement on forensic anthropology.

In accomplishing this rather onerous task, I have been greatly benefit by the discussion I have had time and again with my colleagues, students and friends. I consider this an opportunity to express my gratitude to all of them. My friend and colleague, Vinay Kumar Srivastava has rendered valuable suggestions in the preparation of this manuscript. Dr. V.N. Sehgal, Director, Central Forensic Science Laboratory, C.B.I. New Delhi has put me in his debt by contributing a generous Foreword. I am equally grateful to Dr. P.C. Joshi, Head, Department of Anthropology, Garhwal University, Srinagar, Garhwal and Mr. Anil Mahajan for helping me at various junctures in the completion of this work.

My wife, Ravinder, has been a great source of encouragement, and she has always provided me the most treasured environment in which I could devote myself to the academic pursuits. Meeta, Vinita and Tina, my daughters, have variously helped me while I kept myself engrossed in this endeavour.

Finally, I wish to render my apology to those whose names might have slipped my mind inadvertently.

SURINDER NATH

CONTENTS

CHAPTER 1

INTRODUCTION

Bones form the basic framework of all vertebrate body including *Homo Sapiens* and certain significant information pertaining to man's adaptive mechanisms to his environment. The reconstruction of man's past would almost be impossible without bone as they often survive the process of decay and therefore provide the major evidence of human form after death. Bass (1971) listed following main reasons to the basic question—"Why study bones?"

(a) The bones provide the evidence for the study of fossil man.

(b) They are the basis of racial (ethnic) classification in prehistory.

(c) They are the means of biological comparison of prehistoric people with the present living descendants.

(d) The bones bear witness to burial pattern and provide evidence of culture and world view of the people studied.

(e) They are the major source of information on ancient disease (causing skeletal deformity) and often provide information pertaining to the cause of death.

(f) Their identification usually helps in solving forensic or medico-legal cases.

The study of bones is highly pertinent to a physical anthropologist as he often indulges in reconstructing the man's past and also in identification of the person through bones.

The human skeleton is composed of bones and cartilages. The bones, present in the human body, are of four types, i.e., long, short, flat and irregular.

1. *Long bones* include main components of the two extremities (limbs).
2. *Short bones* include metacarpals of hands, metatarsals of feet, and phalanges of both hands and feet.
3. *Flat bones* include cranial bones, innominates and scapula.
4. *Irregular bones* include vertebra, carpals, tarsals and certain cranial bones.

The human adult possesses 206 bones in all with a slight variation in exceptional cases. Generally there are 806 centres of ossification in the growing skeleton and by maturity these centres have united to form 206 bones of an adult human being (Fig. 1).

While studyng the bones for identification purpose one must be certain that what bone is it ? and to decide whether it is sub-adult or adult bone ? Is it a cranial bone or a post cranial bone ? If it is a cranial bone then one must ascertain whether it is a flat bone or an irregular bone before proceeding further for examination. In case the bone belongs to post cranial skeleton then it is necessary to establish whether it is a long bone (belonging to extremities) or a short bone (metacarpals, metatarsals, phalanges or clavicle), a flat bone (hip bones, scapulae, ribs or sternum) or an irregular bone (vertebrae, carpals, tarsals or patellae).

The skeletal material must be handled with utmost care during examination as it is an important physical evidence in any forensic case. The skeletal material must be packed very carefully in separate bags or cases to avoid mixing of any nature for its proper examination by the forensic anthropologists to establish the sex, age, ethnicity, stature, time and cause of death. Depending upon the circumstances and the material available for examination, forensic anthropolgists are capable

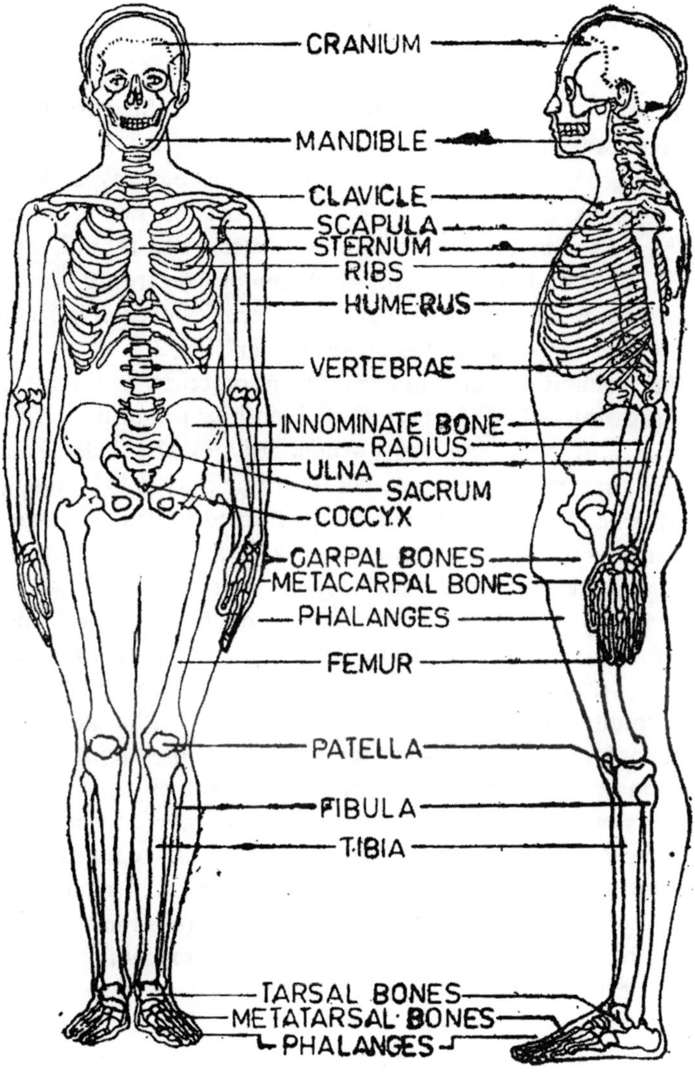

Front View Lateral View

Fig. 1 : Human Skeleton

of establishing more or less complete identity from skeletal material.

A. DEFINITION

Forensic Anthropology, according to T.D. Stewart (1979), is that branch of physical anthropology which, for forensic purposes, deals with the identification of more or less skeletonised remains known to be, or suspected of being, human. Beyond the elimination of nonhuman elements, the identification process undertakes to provide opinions regarding sex, age, race, stature, and similar other characteristics of each individual involved as may lead to his or her recognition.

This definition encompasses certain practices in the forensic field growing out of the fact that identity, primarily, depends on the soft parts and only secondarily, on the skeletal parts. Medical experts or coroners, whose prime duty is to investigate unexplained deaths, are basically trained to deal with fleshed remains. But on confrontation with remains where flesh covering does not help in yielding identification clues, they immediately realize that the only possibility of getting the required information is through the study of skeletons. At this juncture, they often seek help from forensic anthropologists on account of their osteological expertise. Although forensic anthropologists deal with remains that are more or less skeletonised but in many instances the medical examiners or coroners prefer remains that are partly flesh covered when found. The remnants of flesh attached to skeletal remains usually obscure the osteological examination which, in such cases, is possible only after removal of the flesh from the bones. Of all the human dead that require forensic examination, those whose soft parts have deteriorated to the extent that they can be considered more or less skeletonised are a small minority. Thus for this reason forensic anthropology has never been an overworked profession.

The regular occupation of many physical anthropologists involves one or the other activity directed towards gaining greater biological perspective on mankind and since the study of physical man through time is possible only by means of surviving skeletal remains, the physical anthropologists who pursue this line of study obviously acquire extensive knowhow of skeletal anatomy. Thus, anthropological study of a skeleton from the past is more like the forensic study of a skeleton from the present, because the object of study in each case is unknown who must be identified as to sex, age, race, stature, etc. Regardless of purpose, physical anthropologists sharpen their interpretative skill by practicing on collections of documental skeletons from dissecting rooms while forensic anthropologists always deal with the skeletonised remains derived from crime scenes or excavations.

In actual practice identification of human remains for forensic purposes is dominated by forensic pathologists, but is shared according to the circumstances, with other forensic experts. The dependence of forensic anthropologists on medical experts or coroners for a role in forensic identification is very much reflected in various books on legal medicine (Kerley, 1973 ; Krogman, 1962 ; Stewart, 1968, 1973). None of these publications take into account the legal responsibilities of forensic anthropologists or trace the development of the identification procedures they employ. The importance of historical orientation in this instance rests on the verification it has to offer of anthropology's long peripheral relationship to medicine. Thomas Dwight (1843-1911) was the first American to make major contributions to the field and participated in number of forensic cases. On account of the nature of his contributions he was designated as the "father of forensic anthropology" in the United States. He was mainly concerned with a factor that underlies every determination in forensic anthropology, i.e. human variability. The existence of this variability places limits on one's ability to describe in precise terms like age, sex, race and stature, etc. The resulting lack of precision in these matters precludes consideration of forensic anthropology as an exact science.

Forensic identification implies an obligation on the part of experts to the legal system entrusted with the investigation of unexplained deaths. This obligation is fulfilled when a forensic anthropologist files a report of his examination and follows this up by testifying in court. This is why an explanation of the role of expert witness is important for understanding the appropriate way of handling of skeletal material recovered in forensic situations. The handing of bones provide a forensic anthropologist an opportunity to distinguish non-human (animal) from human to decide whether or not the human bones have been altered by exposure to fire, and to size up all signs having a bearing on the cause of, and duration of time since, death. After settling these matters, a forensic anthropologist is ready for examination of specific identification traits.

B. DEATH

The normal functioning of a living body is due to the integrity of three main interdependent systems, viz. (1) circulation, (2) respiration, and (3) innervation, and the failure of any one of them would eventually cause a failure to the remaining two systems. This failure leads to death of an individual. Death, in general, may be defined as complete and persistent cessation of the functions of brain, heart and lungs, the so-called tripod of life. It occurs in two stages, i.e. somatic and molecular. Somatic death is associated with extinction of the personality, while molecular death pertains to the death of individual tissues and it occurs, say, three to four hours after the somatic death.

Somatic Death

This form of death is referred to in common parlance. The time of its occurrence might have legal implications, but the decision as to when death occurred is always a medical one. Its onset is not much difficult to detect provided the dying person has been under observation during the last minutes of life. It is said to have occurred when the last expiration is followed by continued immobility of the chest, loss of pulse, muscular relaxation and alteration of the features. These changes indicate cessation of circulation and respiration and that the nervous system will soon succumb if it has not already done so. Once the co-ordinated contractions have ceased the residual movement of the heart is of no value because these movements are insufficient to maintain the circulation, they can be detected through electrocardiograph (E.C.G.) and will stop within minutes.

The latest development of medical techniques has posed a number of problems with regard to death. Earlier it was accepted that death had occurred if respiration and the circulation ceased for a period of ten minutes, it is now possible to stop the heart and respiration for an hour or more and to restart them again at will through cooling the whole body to 15°C or 59°F. So, during this period of cardiac and respiratory arrest, the E.C.G. and E.E.G. show no electrical activity and the appearance of the body is that of a corpse. This clearly leads to the view that it is not the cessation of the respiration and the circulation that indicates death, but their failure to return.

The doctor, as the final arbiter, must satisfy himself not only that the respiration and heart beat have ceased but that their failure has persisted for such a period that under the specific circumstances it is impossible for the person to regain life.

Molecular Death

The occurrence of clinical death implies the failure of the body as an integrated system. After somatic death, life continues for some time in separate tissues which constitute the body. These tissues die after varying periods depending on the ability of the tissues to function without a blood supply. This is known as molecular or cellular death. Nervous tissue succumbs rapidly, the vital centres of the brain within about five minutes which makes the cardiac arrest dangerous. The muscles live longer and will contract to direct electrical stimulation for nearly three hours after death when post-mortem changes in the fibers indicate the onset of rigor mortis. The corneal reflex and the pupillary light reflex disappear at the time of death, but the instillation of atropine into the eye upto four hours after death will cause some dilatation due to its direct effect on the muscle of the iris and similarly, eserine will causc constriction up to one hour after death.

Recent advances in the treatment procedure makes us fully aware of the fact that we die in bits and pieces. They also emphasises the difficulties inherent in the popular concept of the moment of death.

C. MODES OF DEATH

Bichat (cf. Parikh, 1986) identified three modes of death, i.e. Coma, Syncope and asphyxia, as the proximate causes of death.

A. *Coma* pertains to death due to failure of brain functioning as a result of paralysis of the vital centres. A person may die of compression of the brain due to diseases of the brain or its membranes or due to injuries to the brain. The postmortem will reveal the cause of death as compression from haemorrhage, tumour, gumma, foreign body or vascular lesion and inflammation of the meninges.

B. *Syncope* pertains to death resulting from failure of the functioning of heart. It occurs when death is caused due to heart disease, from haemorrhage, pathological state of the blood or poisoning due to oleander, digitalis or tobacco. The postmortem reveals comparatively little quantity of blood in cavities of the heart, the organs are pale and capillaries are congested.

A syncopal death may occur as a result of reflex cardiac arrest or inhibition of the heart due to vagal stimulation (vasovagal shock). Under this condition, cardiac and respiratory centres are paralysed suddenly with consequent stoppage of heart and respiration which results in sudden loss of life. The vagal stimulation is generally caused due to sudden emotion and injury to receptor areas, such as caroted sinus, testicles, serous membranes, etc.

Vagal stimulation or inhibition as a cause of death is important in cases involving throttling, emotional tension, sudden immersion of the body in cold water, abortion, insertion of an instrument into uterus, bladder, rectum or any body cavity, accidental hanging, etc. Anatomical changes are not observed in all such cases and therefore, no characteristic postmortem appearances are reported.

C. *Asphyxia* is the death caused due to failure of the lung functions. Asphyxia occurs in pathological conditions of the respiratory system like paralysis of the respiratory centre, pneumonia, occlusion of the air passages, and breathing of irrespirable gases. Under these conditions the respiratory function ceases before that of the heart. The postmortem appearances exhibit cyanosis, pronounced lividity, visceral congestion, petechial haemorrhages and cardiac dilatation.

In general it is not possible to certify that a person died of coma, syncope or asphyxia without mentioning the cause that has produced them. Usually the postmortem reports are not very specific and the findings may be similar under different modes of death.

Gorden (cf. Parikh, 1986), on the other hand, is of the opinion that cessation of the vital functions is caused by the deficient supply of oxygen to the tissues (tissue anoxia) that leads to circulatory failure and death. He classified anoxia into following four categories :

1. anoxic anoxia
2. anaemic anoxia
3. histotoxic anioxia, and
4. stagnant anoxia

1. *Anoxic anoxia* pertains to defective oxygenation of blood in lungs. It may be caused due to the following reasons :

(i) *Mechanical interference to the passage of air into the respiratory tract by*

(a) closure of the external respiratory orifices, i.e. nose and mouth,
(b) closure of the air passages by external pressure on the neck as evidenced in strangulation, throttling and hanging,
(c) closure of the air passages by the impact of foreign bodies as evidenced in choking and gagging cases, and
(d) occlusion of the respiratory tract and lungs by fluid in drowning cases.

(ii) *Prevention of normal movements of the chest* as in :

(a) strychnine poisoning,
(b) in traumatic asphyxia from wounds of the thorax, and
(c) due to pressure on the chest in a stampede or a building collapse.

(iii) *Primary cessation of the respiratory movements due to paralysis of the respiratory centre.* The cessation may be caused by

(a) injury or disease, and
(b) in morphine and barbiturate poisoning

(iv) *Breathing rarefied due to* inhalation of carbon dioxide or sewer gas or high altitude climbing or flying.

2. *Anaemic anoxia* pertains to reduction of oxygen carrying capacity of the blood as evidenced in cases of acute haemorrhage or due to acute poisoning by carbon monoxide and nitrites.

3. *Histotoxic anoxia* is caused as a result of depression of oxidative processes in the tissues. As in case of potassium cyanide poisoning the tissue cells are poisoned and thus cannot use the oxygen supplied to them.

4. *Stagnant anoxia* pertains to inefficient circulation through the tissues as observed in cases of heat stroke, shock, cognestive cardiac failure, and corosive poisoning. This categorisation exhibits signs of asphyxia not only in asphyxial deaths due to mechanical interference with respiration but also in other cases of tissue poisoning, acute haemorrhage and natural diseases.

The categorisation of modes of death propounded by Bichat is based on the system indicating death and provides a detailed account of the cause of death while Gordon's classification emphasizes upon the ultimate general changes that cause cardiac failure or death.

D. CHANGES AFTER DEATH

Following changes occur in the body at about the time of death or within minutes after death :

1. Cessation of respiration
2. Cessation of circulation
3. Pallor of the skin
4. Muscular flaccidity
5. Contact flattening and Pallor
6. Eye changes

As the period of death extends into the first and subsequent hours, obvious postmortem changes occur in the body which permit a more certain diagnosis of death. The changes that occur during few hours after death pertain primarily to the muscular tissues of the body.

The muscular tissues of the body after death pass through the following stages, viz. (1) primary relaxation (2) rigor mortis and (3) secondary relaxation, which eventually leads to the skeletonisation of the dead body.

1. **Primary Relaxation**

Under ordinary circumstances, just after death, there is relaxation of muscular tone which rssults in drooping of the lower jaw. The eyeballs lose their tension, the pupils dilate and the muscles become soft and flabby. The joints become flexible, the sphincters relax and there may be incontinence of urine and faeces. As molecular death, i. e. death of tissues and cells, occurs only after there to four hours after somatic death, the muscles react to external stimuli, mechanical or electrical, and the tissues remain alkaline.

2. **Rigor Mortis** (Cadaveric rigidity)

There is a gradual stiffening of the muscles and shortening of the fibers after the period of irritability has passed. The exact changes in the body that leads to stiffening, shortening and opacity of muscles in rigor mortis are not yet known with full certainty. Although the changes are likely to be those which occur during physiological contraction of muscles, but the the ones which occur during rigor are irreversible. The changes are probably due to the breakdown by enzymes of substances in the muscles with the liberation of acid metabolites, like lactic acid. During life time these acid metabolites are carried away by the blood stream, and glycogen is carried to the tissues for the resynthesis of the substances broken down by the enzymes. Resynthesis continues after death for a short time, depending upon the locally available glycogen, but after consumption of the glycogen the acid metabolites accumulate and cause contraction of the muscles. This contraction persists until onset of autolysis. During rigor mortis, the reaction of the muscles changes to acidic from alkaline probably due to the formation of lactic acid. The essential feature of rigor mortis is the altered physical state of the actomyosin caused by gradual exhaustion of adenosine triphosphate (ATP). The actomyosin, a combination of two proteins i. e. myosin and actin, has a remarkable property of contraction and relaxation in the presence of ATP and KCL. After death, the ATP begins to decompose with its decomposition, the actomyosin is gradually converted into a dehydrated stiff gel and results in a condition known as rigor mortis.

Rigor mortis first appears in involuntary muscles, and then in voluntary muscles. It is independent of the nerve supply as it develops in paralysed limbs also. It is tested by gently bending the various body joints.

In voluntary muscles, rigor mortis, as a rule, first appears in the muscles of the eyelids and then in the muscles of face, neck and trunk followed by the muscles of the upper and the lower extremities respectively. The muscles of the fingers and toes are the last to be affected.

When rigor mortis is established, the jaw, neck and the extremities become fixed in position with the arms bent at the elbows and the legs at the knees and hips, and movements at the joint are possible within a very limited range. The rigidity passes off generally in the same order in which it occurred, due to autolysis.

Rigor mortis generally commences within three to six hours after death in temperate climate and may take two to three hours to develop. It may disappear in 18 to 24 hours in summer and by 48 hours in winter. But in temperate regions it usually lasts 2 to 3 dáys.

Rigor mortis *per se* is not reliable for estimating the time of death because it is influenced by a number of factors like (1) age and condition of the body, (2) mode of death, (3) surroundings, (4) freezing or cold stiffening, (5) head coagulation or heat stiffening, and (6) cadaveric spasm, which stimulate rigor mortis. But observations relating to state of rigidity should not be avoided as they may provide supplementary evidence, at times, regarding time of death.

Of all the factors influencing rigor mortis, cadaveric spasm or instantaneous rigor has a considerable legel importance.

This condition is developed only in cases where somatic medico death occurs with extreme rapidity. The spasm is primarily a vital phenomenon and is originated by normal nervous stimulation of the muscles but for some obscure reason, it persists after death. It usually involves groups of muscles only (e. g. of forearm and hands) but in certain cases the whole body is affected. When an object is held in the hand of a person at the time of death, the development of cadaveric spasm may result in this object remaining firmly grasped after death. An object cannot be grasped in this manner during ordinary development of rigor mortis. The contraction of the muscles involved in cadaveric spasm is more pronounced than in the case of rigor mortis, whereas in rigor mortis only a moderate degree of force is required to overcome the muscle stiffness as compared to cadaveric spasm where a great force is required. Moreover, cadaveric spasm does not pass off after two to three days like rigor mortis remains established until putrefactive changes in the muscle groups involved break the concentration.

Following are the major differences between cadaveric spasm and rigor mortis :

Cadaveric spasm	*Rigor mortis*
1. This is the continuation after death of the state of contraction in which muscles were at the instant of death. The stage of primary relaxation is absent. Muscles possess molecular life and therefore respond to stimulation.	1. This is due to changes in muscles after the molecular death of their cells and is preceded by general relaxation of the muscles. Since molecular death has supervened, muscles are irresponsive to stimulation.
2. Death must be sudden and take place whilst the person is in a state of extreme nervous tension	2. Not so.
3. Only certain groups of muscles or all the muscles of a limb or limbs are affected. The involved muscle groups must be in a state of physical activity at the time of death.	3. Every muscle in the body, voluntary, or involuntary, takes part in the process. The condition develops in a certain sequence.

4. The muscle contraction is quite marked and considerable force is required to overcome muscle stiffness.	4. The muscle contraction is less marked and only moderate force is required to overcome the muscle stiffness.
5. Weapon or other article found firmly clutched in the hand of a dead person can be removed with great difficulty. This is a conclusive proof that the object so clutched was gripped at or about the movement of death. It thus helps to indicate the mode of death, whether suicide homicide or accident.	5. Such a state cannot be stimulated by the development of rigor mortis nor can it be produced by any method after death. The changes in rigor mortis after supplementary confirmatory evidence to indicate the time of death arrived at by other means.
6. The muscle contraction remains established until putrefactive changes break the contraction.	6. The muscle contraction passes of after about two to three days or even earlier according to season and climate.

3. Secondary Relaxation

The muscles become soft and flaccid once again with the disappearance of rigor mortis, but do not respond to mechanical or electrical stimuli. The reaction of the muscles again becomes alkaline. This stage is synchronous with the onset of putrefaction.

The late signs represent decomposition and decay or the modification of such process in the dead body and include putrefaction and skeletonisation, adipocere formation and mummification.

(a) Putrefaction

Putrefaction or decomposition is the last stage in the resolution of the body from the organic to the inorganic state and is absolutely a certain sign of death. The breaking down of the tissues is mostly due to the action of micro-organisms, and any condition which favours bacterial growth, accelerates the onset of putrefaction. The main characteristic features of putrefaction are the (i) colour changes and (ii) the development of foul smelling gases.

The primary visible sign of putrefaction is the greenish discolouration of the abdomen over the caecum and the flanks. It may appear as early as within six hours of death during summer and may appear after twenty-four hours or more during winter. This discolouration spreads all over the abdomen and the remaining body within next twenty-four hours. After the spread of discolouration of the skin, the veins of the skin become visible as blue or purplish lines due to the pigment from decomposing blood passing through the vessel walls. This condition of the body is referred to as marbling. It initiates after twenty-four hours and observed prominently in 36-48 hours.

As the abdominal colour changes the body begins to emit a nauseating and unpleasant smell (odour of decay) due to the gradual formation of gases of decomposition. Gas formation is abundant between 24 to 48 hours after death. During this period the body is swollen, bloated and discoloured all over. The face becomes highly bloated due to putrefactive emphysema to such an extent that it becomes difficult to identify. The eyes bulge out of their sockets, the tongue is swollen and protruded. Blebs of gases appear under the skin which has become greenish and the cuticle commences to peel. Wounds, caused before or after death, begin to bleed once more and become so different in appearance that it may be difficult to form an opinion as to whether they were caused before or after death. Observing all these conditions one may conclude that the individual has been dead for more than 36 hours.

Flies are attracted to such putrefying bodies and lay their eggs in the open wounds and natural orifices. Their eggs hatch into maggots in about 24 hours and they crawl into the interior of the body to destroy the soft tissues. Nearly between 4 to 5 days the maggots develop into pupae, which in turn develops into adult flies in another 4 to 5 days. These changes are quite useful in estimating time since death.

Between 48 and 72 hours, the rectum and uterus protrude. Foetus of a pregnant woman may be expelled out of uterus. Loosening of skin, hair and nails occur during this period.

This is followed by loosening of teeth from their sockets and running out of liquefied brain substance through the loosened sutures.

If purtefaction still continues, the liquefied, disintegrated soft tissues separate from bones and fall off. The bones are consequently exposed and the orbits are empty. The body is thus skeletonised. The time consumed by these changes, that lead to the skeletonisation, is variable, depending upon the climatic conditions.

The process of putrefaction slows down when the fatty tissues of the body get converted into fatty acids (adipocere formation) or when the body tissues may become dehydrated (mummification) or when both changes occur simultaneously in different body parts.

Often we find that the rate at which putrefaction occurs is highly variable. This variation is caused due to external and internal factors. The main external factors, which affect the rate of putrefaction are (1) warmth, (2) moisture, (3) air, and (4) manner of burial. While the basic internal factors include (1) age and body condition, (2) sex, and mode of death.

(b) Adipocere Formation

Adipocere formation or saponification is a modified form of putrefaction which is characterised by transformation of certain fatty tissues of the body into a substance known as adipocere. Adipocere formation is mainly caused due to moisture and the process is accelerated by warm temperature and relative diminution of air and micro-organisms. Adipocere is a yellowish white, greasy, wax-like substance which has a rancid odour. It is more or less permanent lasting for several years but turns hard, brittle and yellow when exposed to air. It develops in the subcutaneous tissues and is commonly found in the fatty tissues of the cheeks, breasts and buttocks.

In case the centre for adipocere formation is the facial region, the features are well preserved and when the whole body is involved, the form and contours of the body are well retained to the extent that the wounds inflicted on the body before death may easily be recognized. The duration of time required for formation of adipocere varies greatly. This process is more rapid in infants and bodies of young children as compared to adults. During summer months, its formation may consume nearly three weeks, but it takes between 3 to 6 months for an adult limb and about 12 months for the whole body to be converted into adipocere.

Following are the medico-legal aspects associated to the formation of adipocere.

(i) It helps to establish the identity of a person since the features are well preserved.

(ii) It provides an indication of the cause of death because body injuries are easily recognized.

(iii) It indicates time of death. In India, due to climatic conditions, the adipocere formation generally takes 3 to 6 weeks or even less at times.

(iv) It indicates the place of burial, water or moist ground, from which the body has been recovered.

C. Mummification

It is yet another modified form of putrefaction which is characterised by the dehydration of the tissues and viscera after death. It occurs in conditions that are exactly opposite to those required for adipocere formation. Mummification is not a common condition but may be encountered occasionally in bodies that have been buried in dry soil, like desert sand and in those bodies that have been exposed to warm and dry atmospheric conditions after death. Chronic arsenic or antimony poisoning is said to favour the process of mummification in dry, warm climates. Mummified tissues are hard, dry, shrivelled and often black in colour. The skin adheres closely to the bones and a body in this condition is practically odourless. An important feature of this process is the preservation of the anatomical features of the deceased for many years unless attacked by animals or insects.

The time consumed by the process of mummification varies between 3 months and a year depending upon the body size. This process is much more rapid with the bodies of infants.

Formation of mummification provides following medico-legal informations.

(i) It helps to establish identity of a person as all the features are well preserved.

(ii) Cause of death can be detected as various injuries are easily recognized.

(iii) It indicates time since death. Under Indian climatic conditions the process of mummification may take between one month to one year in certain cases.

(iv) It indicates the burial place, from where the body has been recovered.

A dead body may be mummified artificially for preservation through the process of embalming which involves injecting of embalming fluid (formaldehyde and methyl alcohol) into the large arteries and other body cavities. Embalming preserves the body from destruction by micro-organisms. The investigative role of forensic anthropologists begin only after the body has reached skeletal state or skeletonised.

CHAPTER 2

RECOVERY OF SKELETAL REMAINS

The recovery of skeletal material is best performed by an archaeologist or a trained police officer. The care involved in the recovery of skeletal material varies from expert to expert. It may not be possible for a police officer to devote time that would be required to achieve the skill of an archaeologist due to his other preoccupations. Under these circumstances a trained physical anthropologist should be involved in the process of recovering bones from a site. The bones thus recovered from a burial site or a scene of crime should be collected and packed with utmost care as without bones no data (physical evidence) exists for the forensic or physical anthropologist to work with. The bone or a bone fragment which is missing from the collected lot may be the very part which would have answered certain crucial points such as sex, age, ethnicity and cause of death. In such instances a revisit to the site of discovery or scene of crime may be beneficial in recovering certain missing clues that may lead to fruitful results.

The recovered skeletal material should be treated with preservative—the resin-acetone solution—at the laboratory before further examination with regard to restoration. Special precautions must be observed when the skeletal material under-examination is involved in a forensic problem. Proper records of laboratory examinations should be maintained and retained for their use during court room trial.

It is usually observed that the skin adhering to the bones may have changed its colour on decomposition. Due to decomposition the Caucasian skin may turn dark brown to black, and that of Negroes may turn ash gray. Thus the skin colour proves to be a unsatisfactory method for racial discrimination of skeletal material. Kerley (1973) recommended that the colour of skin may be judged from the amount of melanin granules and melanocytes present in the subcutaneous layer in burned or partially decomposed skin found along with the bones. Similarly hair form is also important in determining the ethnicity (race) of a person, if found on the skin. The tatoo and scar marks are also useful, at times, in establishing identity and if possible the flesh attached to bones should be typed for blood. The next step is to remove the residual flesh from the skeletal material to reduce the remains to bone. The routine examination of the material by a forensic anthropologist is obstructed by the presence of flesh as most of the criteria he examines are in the bone rather than decomposed soft tissue.

The procedure for removing soft tissues involve boiling of the material with detergent, autoclaving and treatment with certain chemicals. Snyder, Burdi and Gaul (1975) suggested a procedure for preparing skeletal material from fixed cadavers or partially decomposed remains. The procedure demands preparation of a chemical solution the Antiformin by combining 150 grams of Sodium Carbonate ($NaCO_3$) with 250 ml of water and 100 grams of Bleaching powder with 750 ml of water. Both these solutions are mixed and stirred for three to four hours. To this mixed solution one litre of 15 per cent Sodium Hydroxide (NaOH) is added. After removing the main soft tissue mass surrounding the bone, it is placed in a tank of Antiformin. For quick results the solution may be heated slightly below the boiling point and the temperature is maintained for three to sixty minutes depending on how fast the soft tissues separate out from the bone. The bone is then taken out to brush away the debris. Care has to be taken because a bone will be attacked by Antiformin on prolonged immersion. After cleaning the bone may be degreased in Benzol for twenty four to forty eight hours and then bleached in 3 per cent Hydrogen Peroxide (H_2O_2) or Potassium Hydroxide (KOH) for about twenty four hours. The Antiformin solution can be filtered and reused again for several times by adding occasionally a little fresh Antiformin.

In order to remove the tanacious intervertebral discs the spine is immersed in a tank of Trichloroethane for two to three days, rinse it thoroughly in water and soak in Hydrogen Perxoide for same duration of time. Through this process the discs would be easily separable without any additional treatment and the vertebrae would automatically be bleached.

The available teeth from the skeletal material should also be properly preserved as a forensic odontologist would extract significant information, from teeth on examination, regarding age.

After systematic recovery and cleaning of the bones the forensic anthropologist, with his or her expertise in anatomy and physical anthropology, initiates a proper examination of the skeletal material. The inferences drawn thereform provides useful information pertaining to sex, age race (ethnicity), stature reconstruction, time and cause of death, etc. which can be suitably used for establishing identity and other medico-legal purposes.

On many occasions, the human remains are recovered in decomposed or mutilated form. A careful examination of such remains may yield important information about the deceased.

Examination of Decomposed Remains

Whenever a body exhibits putrefactive changes in varying degree due to the time elapsed since death, it is categorised as a decomposed body. Detection of bone fractures and haemorrhage is possible in such bodies by an expert during post-mortem. The expert can reveal relevant information at autopsy regarding identification and cause of death. At times the decomposed body may be infested with maggots or soil and clothes. Such bodies should be immersed in a tank containing a dilute Carbolic solution (Lysol) to get the clothing away and soften the earth. The maggots infesting the body should be removed before its immersion in Lysol because it kills the maggots. The maggots are useful in estimating time since death through their development.

Identification of a decomposed body is possible by examining the remnants of bones, hair and teeth which resist putrefaction and help in determining the sex and age. The finger skin may provide fingerprints which can help in establishing complete identity. The colour and form of hair, on examination, may disclose identity. The teeth by virtue of their characteristic features may prove to be useful in revealing identity of the deceased. Other peculiarities like tatoo marks, scar marks and malunited bone fractures, etc. may also be of some use in this regard. Besides these the personal property, like clothing, watch, ring, bracelets, etc. of a dead body also provide useful information regarding the deceased.

CHAPTER 3

IDENTIFICATION OF SKELETAL REMAINS

A. IDENTIFICATION OF REMAINS

Identification of human skeletal remains is a crucial matter and a specialist in this field must be well versed in comparative anatomy (osteology, osteometry and craniometry) and racial morphology. In order to identify a single lot of bones, one must be able to fit it accurately into a tremendous jigsaw puzzle within the total range of variations (Krogman, 1962). The growing field of forensic anthropology is now all set to systematize the multifactorial problem of human skeletal reconstructions ushering in new dimensions to include more specific manifestations rendered towards the skeletal remains through the nature of death. Deaths, as a forensic expert classifies, are of three types : (1) natural, (2) accidental, and (3) intentional (Williams, 1976). In cases where a subject has died of natural death, the scientific investigations have less investigatory importance than reporting the pathological rudiments of diseases, bone deformities and anatomical abnormalities. But in cases of accidental deaths caused by train mishap, air crash, road accidents and natural calamities, like earth quakes, typhoons etc., the observations on such multitudes of skeletal wealth with common skeletal manifestations would equip one to formulate the source of disaster. The most important form of death from the forensic standpoint is the intentional death, where the subject is liquidated through homicide or suicide. While dealing with surface finds it is doubtful that a forensic anthropologist can learn more from examining the remains *in situ* than a trained forensic pathologist can, but with buried remains a forensic anthropologist with experience in modern archaeology has a distinct advantage. Forensic investigators tend to be negligent not only in applying archaeological techniques to the recovery of buried remains, but also in making sure that they have recovered all parts of the skeletonised remains discovered above ground. In the latter situation the investigators may fail to look for or recognise certain less conspicuous bones that may have become mixed with the underlying dirt, leaves or debris, sometimes scavenging animals may have carried some of the bones away from the main skeleton. It is quite frustrating while examining skeletal remains to discern that some of the bones are missing. A forensic anthropologist should make sure that he or she has not overlooked anything that may have surrounded the bones before packing the material for transportation to the laboratory.

Failure to recover skeletal material *in situ* and to participate in their removal from the site to the laboratory is advantageous to a forensic anthropologist because it forces him or her to characterise the decendent objectively on the basis of bones alone.

In most cases the remains that are presented to forensic anthropologists for examination are often skeletonised, thus the removal of tissue remnants and adherent extraneous matter is necessary for convenient handling and for exposure of the details that provide the basis for required determinations.

It would be a serious error to clean the bones without noting the location and amount of the tissue remnants, the intensity of odour of decay, the various types of adherent extraneous matter, because everything that is associated with the bones is evidence as to how the remains reached that particular state, and in how much time. The head or the body hair adherent to the bones may reveal on examination, the race of the decendent. The skeletal remains are helpful in identification of the victim, the nature and the mode of death, and also the *modus operandi* adopted by the criminal. In number of instances the dead bodies may be recovered in mutilated form. Mutilation of the dead body is either done by criminal to destroy all traces of identity and thus facilitate the disposal of the dead (Stewart, 1968), or it may be caused by the vultures, jackals, hyenas and dogs. In India one may come across mutilated unclaimed dead bodies of lunatics, fakirs or pilgrims lying on road side or in remote spots (Modi, 1977). Whenever skeletal remains are recovered by law enforcing agencies, these are sent for forensic examinations. During examination of skeletal remains the following key questions may arise (Modi 1977 ; Chaurasia, 1984 ; Nath, 1987).

1. Whether the bones are human or non-human ?
2. Whether they belong to one or more than one individuals ?
3. What would be the sex ?
4. What is the age ?
5. What is the ethnic group (race) of the individual ?
6. How tall the person would be ?
7. What is the cause of death ?
8. What is the time of death ?
9. What are the distinguishing characteristics in the skeletal remains that may lead to personal identification ?

A forensic anthropologist tries to arrive at sex, age, race, stature, etc. in general from skeletal material. For example, if the skeleton in question can be said to be male, the search for identity is reduced to half the population, and if age could also be judged to be around 30 years, the search is further narrowed down to those males who are around that age. Thus, none of these traits alone, nor all of them together, positively identify the individual. But when these traits fit both description of a missing person and the circumstantial evidence connected with the recovery of the skeletal remains, the identification becomes more plausible. Besides general traits the specific traits or individual characteristics like dental anomalies, healed fractures or mastoid air-cell patterns, etc., are unlikely to be matched in any other individual, like fingerprints in fleshed remains. However, identification of a skeletonised individual from one or more specific traits depends upon the favourable comparison with a record made during lifetime, as in the case of fingerprints.

B. HUMAN AND NON-HUMAN BONES

In order to ascertain whether the bones in question are human or non human, it is a matter of establishing the *Corpus delicti* (Cornwall, 1956 ; Stahl, 1980). All bones in fragmentary state may look alike to a untrained person. However, it is casy to identify a human skull through its structure and absence of snout and larger cranial part (Brothwell, 1965 ; Bass, 1971). The species of bone's origin can be determined by precipitation test if organic material is still present (Stewart, 1948 ; Modi, 1977 ; Chaurasia, 1983).

In case of burned bones, the differentiation between human and non-human bones is possible through chemical analysis of bone ash (Krogman, 1948 ; Trotter and Peterson, 1955).

C. ATTRIBUTION OF NUMBER OF INDIVIDUALS

To establish the fact whether the bones recovered represent one or more than one individual, the sorting technique is employed where similar bones are sorted and counted. The determination of side (right or left) is quite useful in such an examination. The recovery of duplicate and/or unmatching bones may help in determining whether they belong to one or more than one individual (Hooton, 1943 ; Snow, 1948 ; Brues, 1958).

CHAPTER 4

ATTRIBUTION OF SEX

Margin of error in sex determination examination varies depending upon the skeletal material available (Giles and Elliot, 1963). In a complete skeleton of a sub-adult the attribution of sex may be a little better than a guess, i.e. around 50 per cent (Brues, 1958) as sex can be more accurately determined after the attainment of puberty (Bass, 1979). The sex differences are well marked in pelvis and skull, thus an accurate determination of sex can be performed in over ninety per cent cases using only pelvis and skull (Krogman, 1962 : Modi, 1977), while in their absence it is somewhat speculative.

Early artistic drawings of human skeleton state that anatomists long have recognised the postmortem persistence of sexual dimorphism in the adult bones and have represented it mainly through distinctions in pelvic conformations. Since the remarkable secondary sex character of the adult female skeleton is the modification of the pelvis for child bearing. The resulting sex differences have been cited as the best indicators of sex in skeleton. Recognition of other sex related traits of skeleton has come into existence more recently. At present the forensic anthropologists have at their disposal a variety of indicators of sex to aid them in their identification efforts although with rare exceptions they are applicable to adults only. Following are the commonly used indicators of sex discrimination in a skeleton.

A. CRANIAL SKELETON

Females while progressing towards adulthood from puberty retain much of the gracility and smoothness characteristic of the prepubertal period, while the male's skull becomes less gracile (Fig. 2). These differences are reflected in the orbital

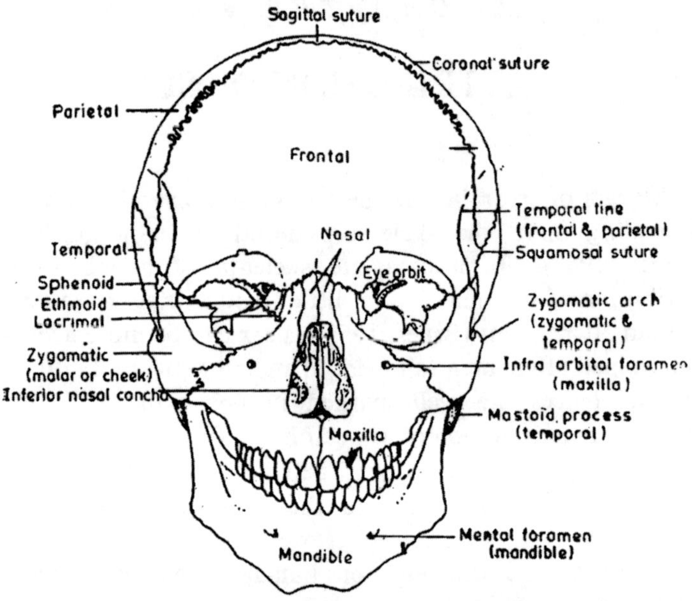

Fig. 2 : Anterior View of Human Skull

margins, supra-orbital ridges, mastoid processes, cheek bones and chin of the lower jaw. Despite the observed variations in the borders, ridge processes and crests the differences are not easily quantified (Table 1). Giles (1970) employed discriminant function analysis for sexing through cranial (Figs. 3 and 4) or mandibular traits (Figs. 5, 6a and 6b) and achieved an accuracy in sexing between 83.2 per cent and 88.3 per cent for American Blacks and Whites depending upon the particular race (ethnic group) involved and the combination of measurements used.

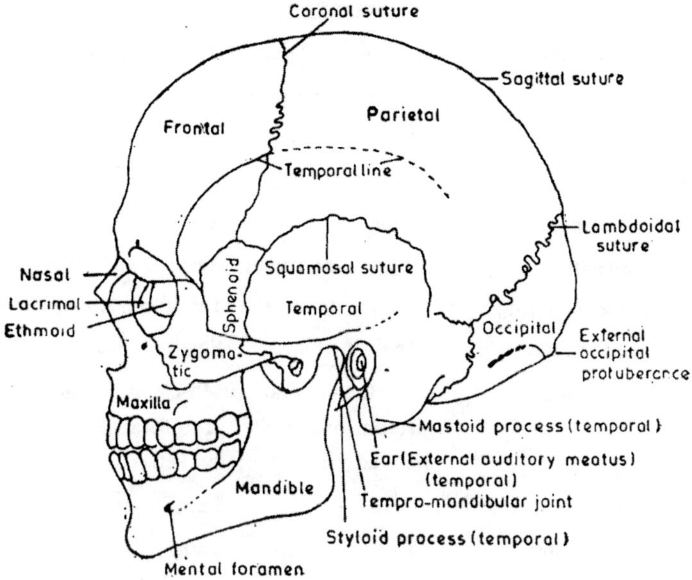

Fig. 3 : Lateral View of Human Skull

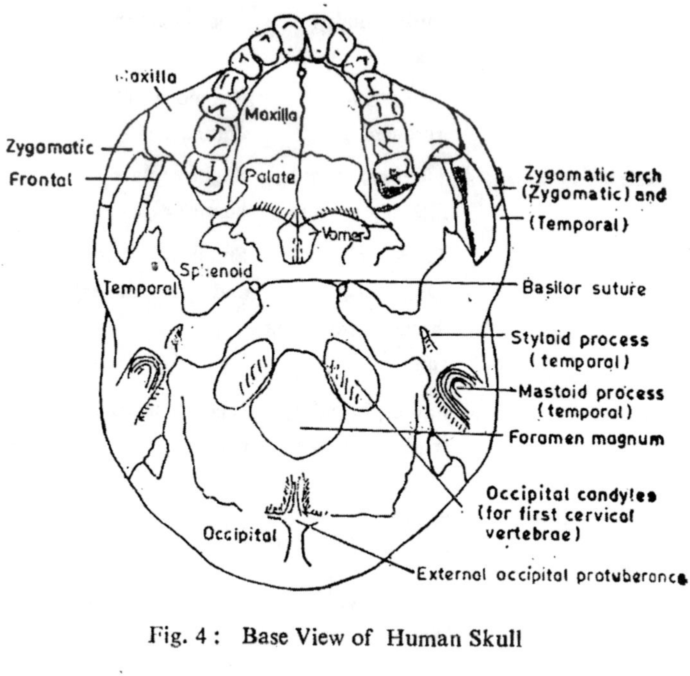

Fig. 4 : Base View of Human Skull

TABLE 1

Common Cranial Traits used for Discrimination of Sex

Sl. No.	Cranial Trait	Male	Female
1.	General size	Large	Small
2.	Architecture	Rugged and rough	Smooth and gracile
3.	Supra-orbital ridges	Medium to large	Small to medium
4.	Mastoid processes	Medium to large	Small to medium
5.	Occipital area	Muscle lines and protuberance well marked	Muscle lines and protuberance not marked
6.	Frontal eminences	Small	Large
7.	Parietal eminences	Small	Large
8.	Orbits	Squared, lower, relatively smaller, with rounded margin	Rounded, higher relatively larger with sharp margins
9.	Forehead	Steeper, less rounded	Rounded full, infantile
10.	Cheek bones	Heavier, more laterally arched	Lighter, more compressed
11.	Mandible	Larger, higher symphysis, broader ascending ramus	Small with less corpal and ramal. dimensions
12.	Palate	Larger, broader, tends more to U-shape	Smaller, tends more to parabola
13.	Occipital Condyles	Large	Small
14.	Teeth	Large, lower Molar 1, more often 5-cusped	Small, molars most often 4-cusped

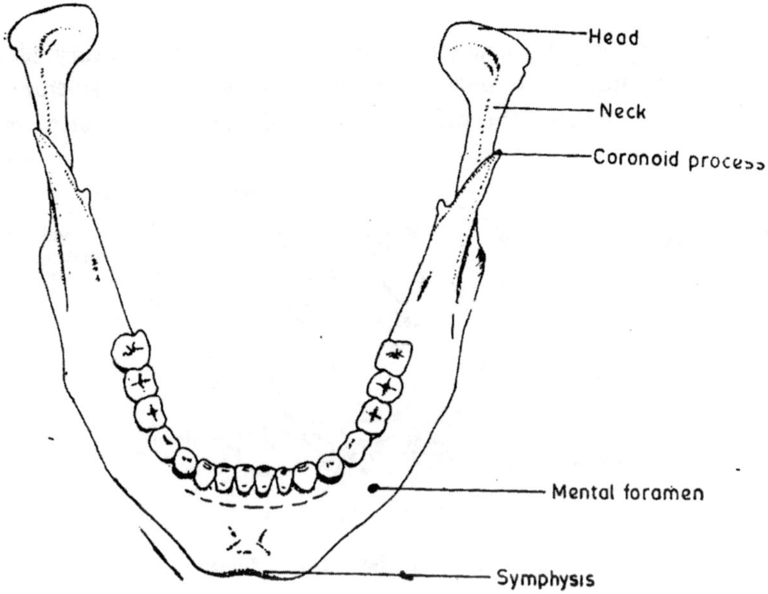

Fig. 5: Human Mandible Viewed From Above

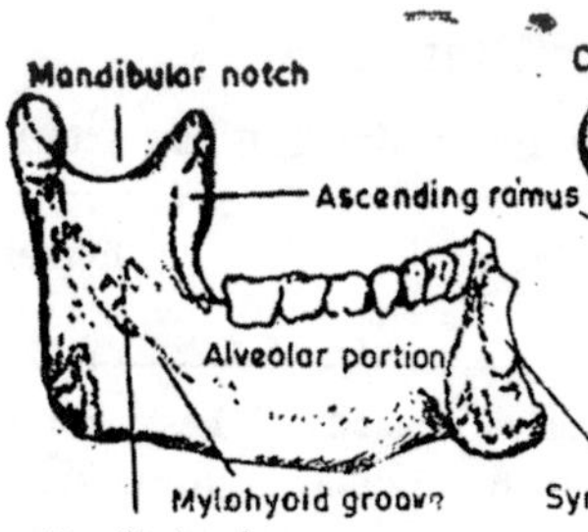

Fig. 6a : Lateral View of Mandible

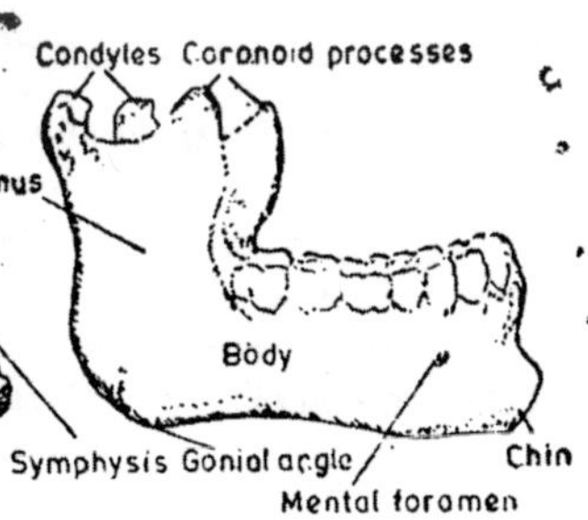

Fig. 6b : Medial Surface of The Left Half of The Mandible

Careful examination of the aforecited traits in their entirety should give a fairly accurate estimate of sex in adult skulls. As several of these criteria are age dependant, the discription of sex differences must, therefore, be limited between 20 and 55 years.

B. POST CRANIAL SKELETON : PELVIS

Forensic test books from the early nineteenth century place reliance upon the pelvis for the attribution of skeletal sex (Fig. 7). Besides the measurements of the pelvic inlet, two

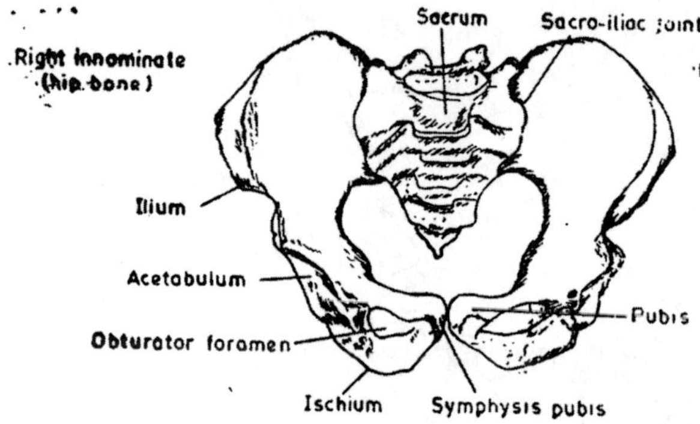

Fig. 7 : Anterior View of the Female Pelvis

main features are often incorporated i.e. (1) sub-pubic angle, and (2) greater sciatic notch. Von Fehling (1876) and Thomson (1899) recognised that the shape of the sciatic notch was different in two sexes during fetal stage (Table 2). Thus,

TABLE 2

Common traits used for discriminating sex from pelvis

Sl. No.	Traits	Male	Female
1.	Pelvis as a whole	Massive, rugged, marked muscular sites	Less massive, gracile, smoother
2.	Symphysis	Higher	Lower
3.	Sub-pubic angle	V-shaped, sharp angle	U-shaped, rounded, broader divergent obtuse angle
4.	Obturator foramen	Large, often ovoid	Small, triangular
5.	Acetabulum	Large, tends to be directed laterally	Small, tends to be directed antero-laterally
6.	Greater sciatic notch	Small, close, deep	Large, wider, shallower

7.	Ischiopubic rami	Slightly everted	Strongly everted
8.	Sacro-iliac articulation	Large	Small, oblique
9.	Preauricular sulcus	Not frequent	More frequent, better developed
10.	Ilium	High, tends to be vertical	Lower, laterally divergent
11.	Sacrum	Longer, narrower with evenly distributed curvature, often 5+segments	Shorter, broader with tendency to marked curve at S. 1-2 and S. 3-5, 5 segments only
12.	Pelvic brim	Heart shaped	Circular or elliptical
13.	True pelvis	Relatively smaller	Oblique, shallow, spacious.

it may be stated that with the exception of the shape of greater sciatic notch, all the osteological sex indicators considered apply to adults. (Figs. 8a, 8b, 9a and 9b).

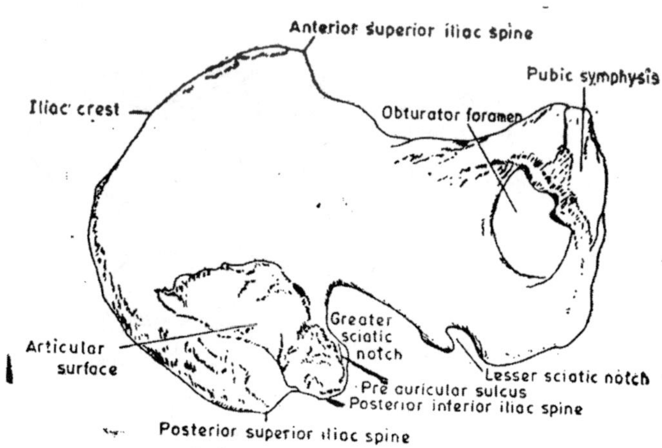

Fig. 8a : Medial View of Left Hip Bone

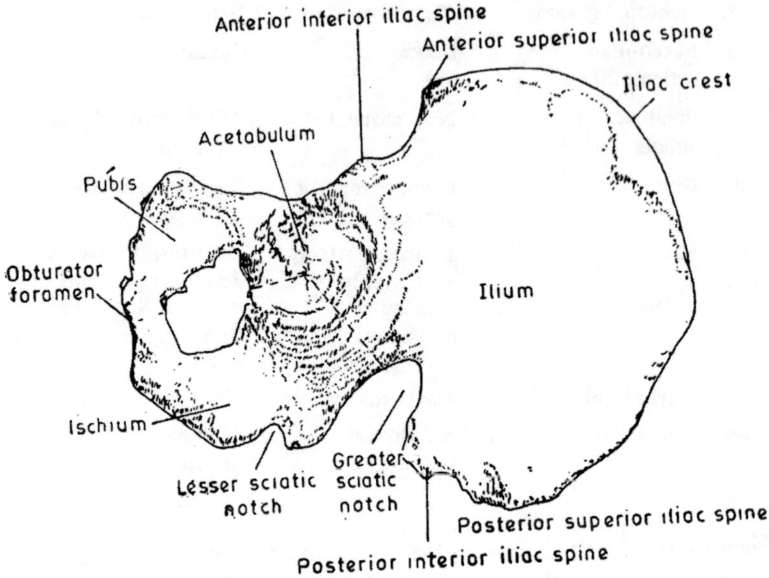

Fig. 8b : Lateral View of Left Hip Bone

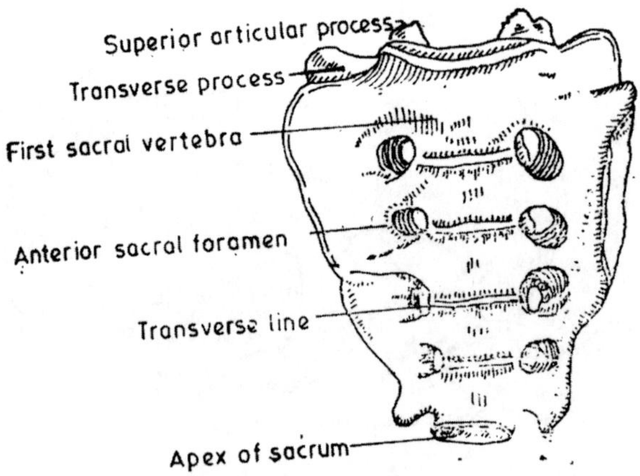

Fig. 9a : Anterior View of Sacrum

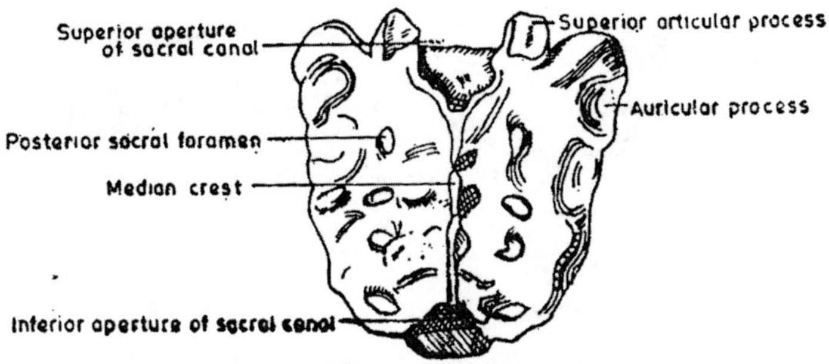

Fig. 9b : Posterior View of Sacrum

Aforecited observations provide a fairly accurate estimate of sex. Pelvis alone can be used to attribute sex of the skeleton to an accuracy of around 95 per cent. This accuracy can be enhanced to up to 99 per cent on considering pelvis in combination with skull.

C. ESTIMATION OF SEX FROM POSTCRANIAL BONES OTHER THAN PELVIS

Generally speaking male limbs are usually longer and robust, the shoulders are broad, the hands and feet longer than the females in living condition. The same applies to the bones of these parts excepting a few cases where females are as robust with broad shoulders as males.

1. *Clavicle* : The clavicle is a bone in which sex differences appear to be fairly well marked but their quantification is not possible. Thieme (1957) used Negro clavicles to determine sex and observed that male clavicles are usually longer with only moderate overlap. Jit and Singh (1966) are of the opinion that the clavicular weight is more valuable in determining sex of males, but not females (Fig. 10). They further commented that the mid-shaft circumference is the single most diagnostic sexual feature of this bone in males only.

2. *Humerus* : The humerus is generally more robust in males than females. Dorsey (1897) commented that if the maximum diameter of the humeral head among Americans measure 44 mm, the chances are extremely great that it is a male bone and if it measures 45 mm than it is a male to a

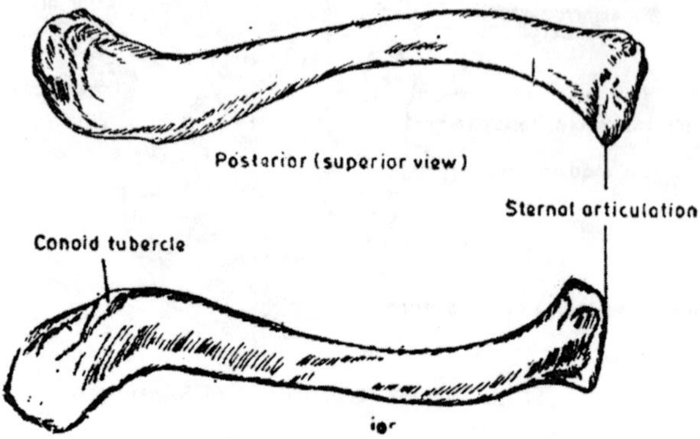

Fig. 10 : The Left Clavicle

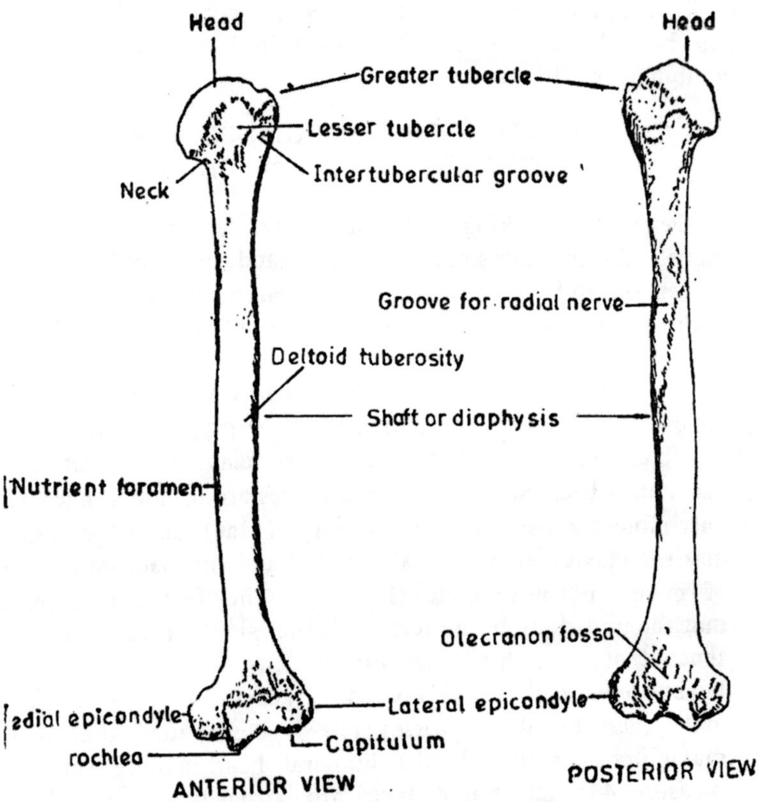

Fig. 11 : The Left Humerus

practical certainty. Thomas Dwight (1904-05) on the basis of vertical and transverse diameter of the head found that these diameters are greater in males than in famales. (Fig. 11).

Measurement	Males	Females
Vertical diameter	48.76 mm	42.67 mm
Transverse diameter	44.66 mm	36.98 mm

Thieme (1957) used epicondylar breadth for sex determination and reports that this breadth is below 56.7 mm for females and is usually above 63.4 mm for males. Oliver (1969), on the other hand listed following data for determining sex from incompletely macerated humeri.

Measurement	Female, if below	Male, if above
1. Maximum length	280 mm	330 mm
2. Vertical diameter of the head with cartilage	43 mm	48 mm
3. Transverse diameter of the head with cartilage	40 mm	44 mm
4. Bone weight	98 gm	136 gm

These figures apply exclusively to Europeans. Oliver further mentions that any individual falling in between these figures may belong to either sex. Stewart (1979) suggests on the basis of vertical diameter of humeral head that females exhibit a value less than 43 mm while males beyond 47 mm.

3. *Ulna*

On the basis of the observations on French ulna, Oliver (1967) provides following figures for sex determination (Fig. 12).

Measurement	Female, if below	Male, if above
Maximum length	230 mm	265 mm
Physiological length	205 mm	240 mm
Bone weight	40.5 gm	54 gm

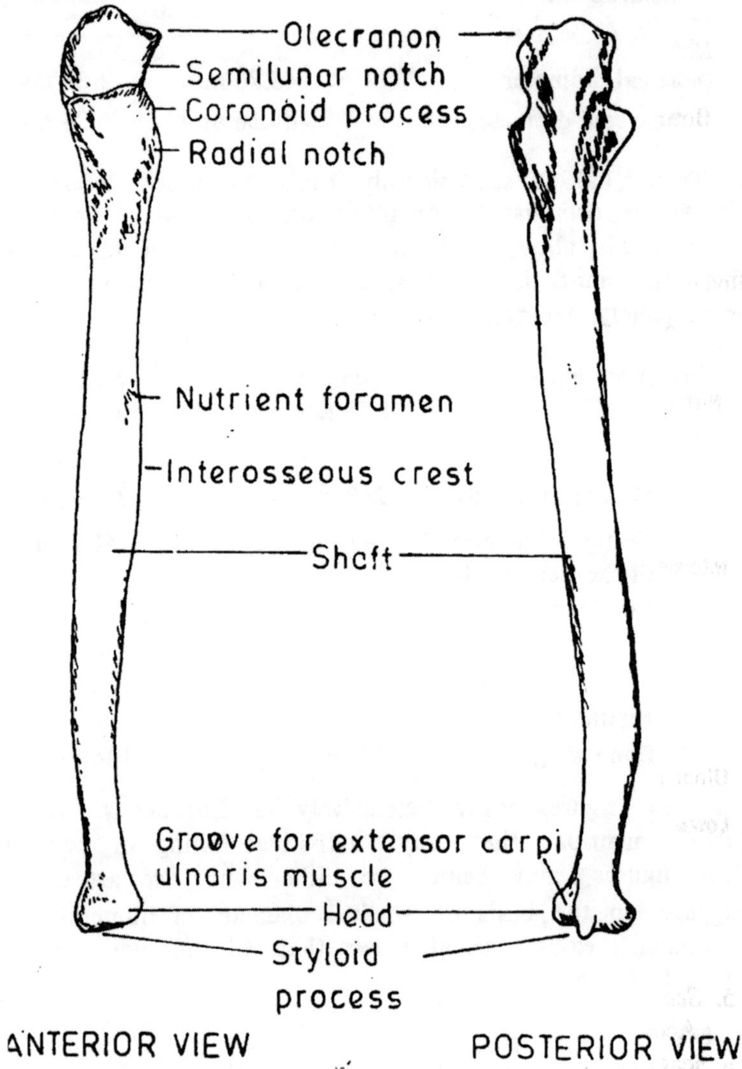

Fig. 12 : The Left Ulna

4. *Radius*

Like ulna, the following dimensions on radius (Fig. 13) have also been reported on French radius by Oliver (1969).

Measurement	Female, if below	Male, if above
Maximum length	215 mm	250 mm
Physiological length	200 mm	235 mm
Bone weight	31 gm	44 gm

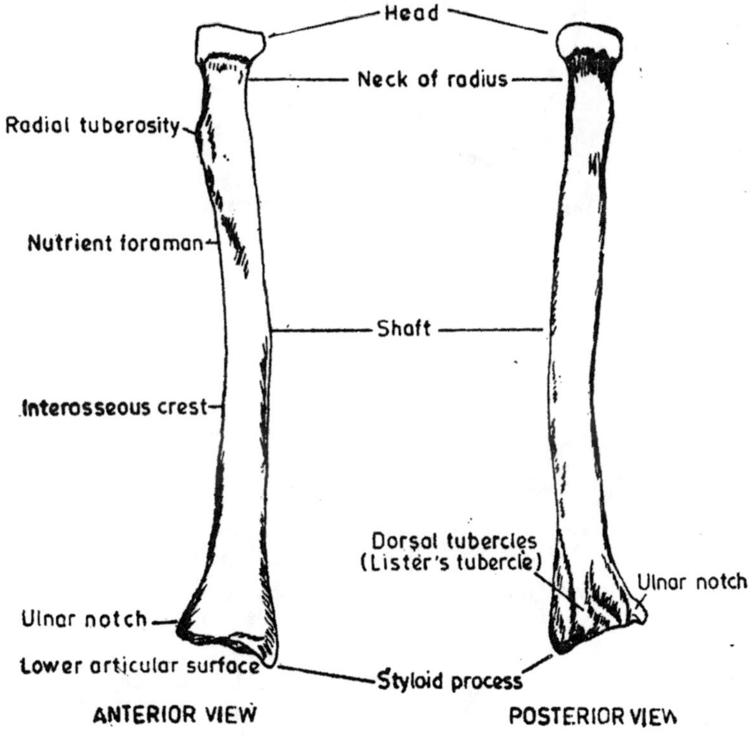

Fig. 13 : The Left Radius

5. *Scapula*

According to Dwight (1894) there is no single instance of a scapula measuring less than 14 cm being identified as male, nor of one measuring 17 cm being female (Figs. 14a and 14b). Stewart (1979) supported the claim of Dwight on both Black

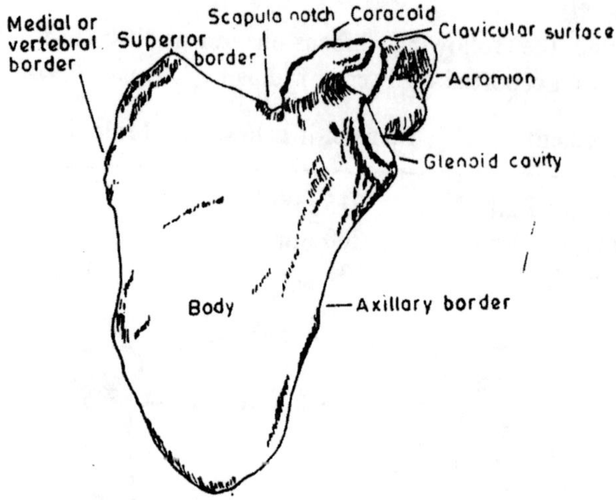

Fig. 14a : Anterior View of Left Scapula

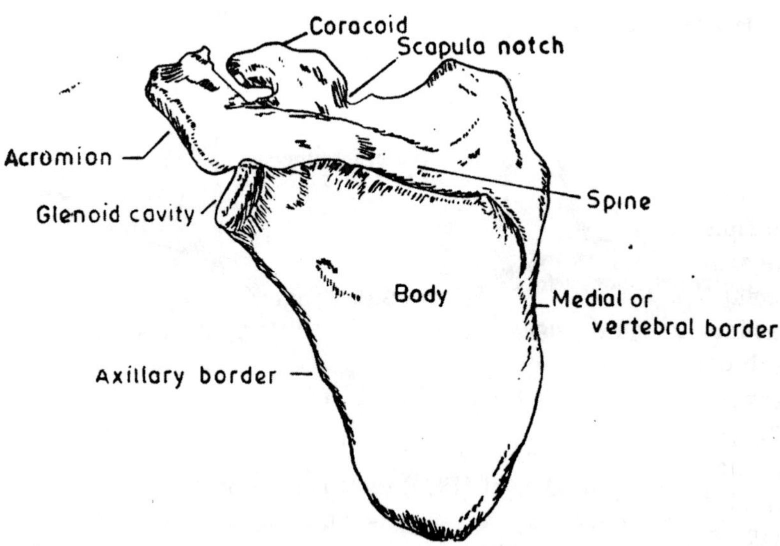

Fig. 14b : Posterior View of Left Scapula

and White Americans (Terry Collection). According to Oliver and Pineau (1957) the following measurements of scapula are helpful in sex determination.

Measurement	Female, if below	Male, if above
Breadth of glenoid fossa	26.1 mm	28.6 mm
Length of spine	127.9 mm	141.4 mm
Infra spinous height of the scapula.	144.4 mm	157.5 mm

6. *Sternum*

It has often been observed that the body of the male sternum is more than twice the length of the manubrium, while among females it is less than twice that length (Joseph Hyrtl, 1865). While according to Dwight (1881) the body of the sternum is usually twice as long as the manubrium in women and two and one-half times as long in men. Hintzshe (1924) and Jit et al. (1980) have also reported similar observations regarding sex differences in sternum.

7. *Femur*

Dwight (1878) specified two points of sexual significance in femur, i.e. (1) among females the long axis of the neck forms an angle close to 90 degrees with the shaft, and (2) when the femur is held with its condyles resting on a level, the shaft inclines further outward than in man ; because women have a broader pelvis and at the same time shorter legs, this arrangement is necessary in order to bring the knees together. Dorsey (1897) confirmed the importance of femoral head in sex determination as in case of humerus. While Stewart (1979) is of the opinion that there is no sexual significance of the angle between the neck and the shaft (Fig. 15).

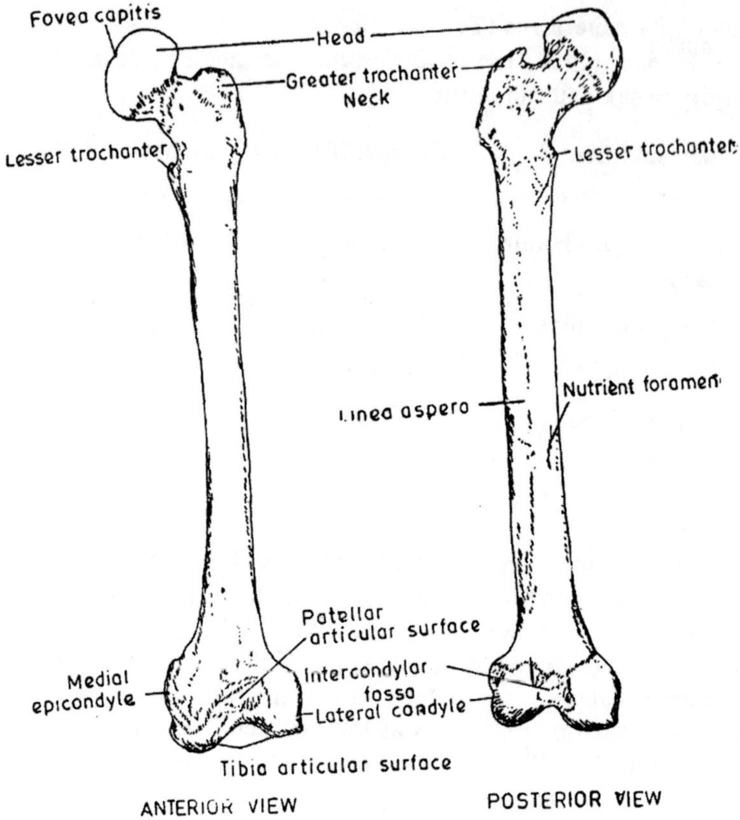

Fig. 15 : The Left Femur

Pearson (1917-19) provided the following estimates for both the sexes on the basis of certain measurements on femur taken in millimetres.

Measurements	Female	Female?	Sex?	Male?	Male
1. Vertical diameter of head	41.5	41.5-43.5	43.5-44.5	44.5-45.5	45.5
2. Popliteal length	106.0	106.0-114.5	114.5-132.0	132.0-145.0	145.0
3. Bicondylar breadth	72.0	72.0-74.0	74.0-76.0	76.0-78.0	78.0
4. Trochantric oblique length	390.0	390.0-405.0	405.0-430.0	430.0-450.0	450.0

Thieme (1957) provided the following figures for Negro femora

Measurement	Female	Male
Femur length	439.10 mm	477.34 mm
Head diameter	41.52 mm	47.17 mm

Oliver (1969) presented following values for European femora on the basis of following measurements

Measurement	Female, if below	Male, if above
Length in position	390.0 mm	460.0 mm
Vertical diameter of head with cartilage	43.5 mm	44.5 mm
Bicondylar breadth	74.0 mm	76.0 mm
Weight	270.0 gm	370.0 gm.

Besides these many other researchers, like, Ignalls (1924), Reid (1927), Hrdlicka (1932), Walemsley (1933), Siddiqui (1934) Hosimota (1938), Pick *et al.* (1941), Khan (1959), Kate (1964). Garn (1972), Singh and Singh (1972 ; 1973 ; 1974) and Black (1978), have contributed a lot to the study of femur bone with regard to determination of sex.

8. *Tibia*

On observing the French sample Oliver (1969) gave following figures regarding length and weight of tibia to discriminate sexes (Fig. 16).

Measurement	Female, if below	Male, if above
Maximum length	320.0 mm	380.0 mm
Weight	156.0 gm	234.0 gm.

9. *Smaller bones of lower extremity*

On the basis of the volume of patella, talus and calcaneus, El-Najjar and McWilliams (1978) provided following figures for determination of sex for Caucasian, Negro and unknown samples (Fig. 17).

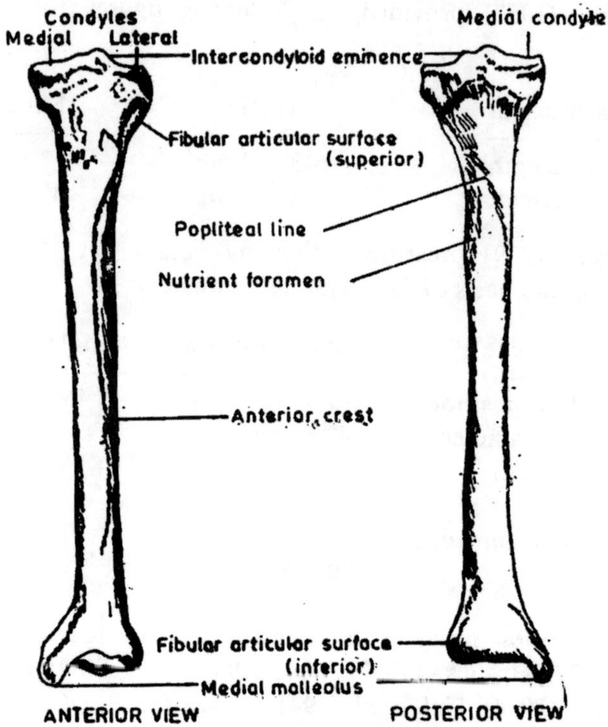

Fig. 16 : The Left Tibia

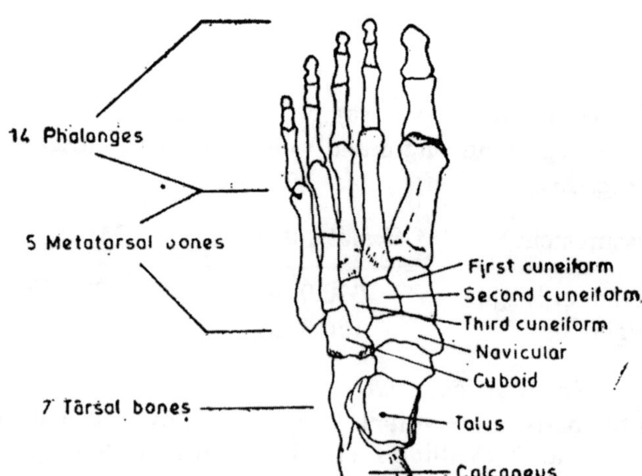

Fig 17 : Skeleton of Human Foot (Left)

Population	Male, if volume is greater than	% error	Female, if volume is less than	% error
A. PATELLA				
1. Caucasian	15 cc	4	14 cc	4
2. Negro	13 cc	6	11 cc	8
3. Unknown	15 cc	3	11 cc	3
B. TALUS				
1. Caucasian	31 cc	4	26 cc	4
2. Negro	33 cc	4	23 cc	4
3. Unknown	32 cc	3	24 cc	3
C. CALCANEUS				
1. Caucasian	55 cc	4	52 cc	6
2. Negro	58 cc	6	50 cc	4
3. Unknown	58 cc	3	50 cc	2

Different researchers have proposed quantitative methods for estimation of sex from skull or post-cranial skeleton (Giles, 1964 ; Boulinier, 1968 ; 1969 ; Giles and Elliot, 1963 ; Hanihara, 1958 ; 1959) in doubtful cases in lieu of observational methods. Lately, Kinzely (1974) propounded a chemical method for assessing sex from fairly fresh bones.

10. *Vertebrae*

The following characters of the cervical and lumbar vertebrae may, at times, help in discerning the sex.

	Male	*Female*
1.	Average breadth of the first cervical vertebra is around 83 mm.	Average breadth of the first cervical vertebra is around 72 mm
2.	The lumbar convexity towards the front (lordosis) is less prominent	The lumbar convexity towards the front (lordosis) is more prominent

11. *Thorax*

In a similar manner the thorax can also help in determining the sex of a skeleton on observing following aspects.

	Male	*Female*
1.	The thoracic cage is longer and narrower.	The thoracic cage is shorter and wider.
2.	The ribs show a lesser curvature and are less oblique in their placement.	The ribs show a greater curvature and are more oblique in their placement.
3.	The body of the sternum is bigger and is more than twice the length of the manubrium.	The body of the sternum is smaller and is less than twice the length of manubrium.
4.	The upper border of the sternum is usually on level with the lower part of the body of the second thoracic vertebra.	The upper border of the sternum is usually on level with the lower part of the body of the third thoracic vertebra.

These aforecited observations on vertebrae and the thoracic cage may be of use in determining sex in absence of important skeletal parts like pelvis and skull.

In general, sexing of unknown skeletal material depends upon relative completeness of the skeleton. In a complete skeleton of a sub-adult the sex determination may be a little better than a guess, i.e. around 50 per cent (Brues, 1958) as sex can be determined more accurately after attainment of puberty (Bass, 1979). The sexual differences are well marked during adult age only, therefore 100 per cent accuracy in sex determination could be achieved, if the skeleton is complete, 90 per cent with skull alone, 95 per cent with pelvis alone, and 98 per cent with skull and pelvis together. The accuracy reduces to 80 per cent when only long bones are considered, but it increares to 90-95 per cent on considering skull with long bones and over 95 per cent when long bones are considered with pelvis for this purpose. These estimates are based on morphometric and morphological observations which, in a skeleton, may differ with the population samples involved. As a general rule, standards should be used with reference to the group from which they are drawn and upon which they are based as they are ordinarily not interchangeable.

CHAPTER 5

DETERMINATION OF AGE

From conception to adulthood, growth and development constitute a major phenomenon of aging. Following the cessation of growth around 23-25 years, depending upon the sex, aging continues in the form of degenerative change, i.e. the estimation of age in the skeleton depends upon different sorts of evidence in each period of life.

Forensic anthropologists generally consider various facts regarding mortality rates at birth into account while dealing with small human remains recovered under suspicious circumstances. The foetuses that attract attention of forensic anthropologists are in such deteriorated state that only after reducing the remains to clean, dry bones, can a safe estimate of size and age, be made. In such cases they do look for evidence relating cause of death and make efforts to establish age at death incorporating their knowledge of bone size at birth. Various signs of development available in preadult skeletal remains to appraise and to relate to age consists of ossification centres of three types.

(i) *Primary centres*, which unite to give major elements of bones their ultimate form.

(ii) *Secondary centres*, that appear at articular ends or margins of various bones and develop into epiphyses.

(iii) *Dental germs,* that appear in special crypts (alveoli) in the jaws and develop into deciduous or permanent teeth.

Krogman (1939) contributed to anatomical knowledge by providing precise information regarding appearance of primary centres of ossification between birth and five years of age. Forensic anthropologists are aware of the fact that skeleton of a new born child includes many bones which are separated into two or more parts derived from primary ossification centres, for example frontal bone is still divided along the midline, each vertebra, excepting axis, consists of a central and two lateral parts, the innominate is represented by the forerunners of the ultimately conjoined ilium, ischium, and pubis. The skull bones of an infant are so thin that they tend to wrap on drying, but that even when not wrapped they articulate imperfectly, showing gaps (fontanelles) in the areas where three or more bones will eventually come together, with two exceptions, the primary centres that have not united at birth will do so during the first six to eight years of post-natal life. The two exceptions are the primary elements of the innominate and the spheno-occipital synchondrosis (basilar suture) where fusion takes place around 20 years.

A. Estimation of Age During Different Developmental Stages

Assessment of age from human skeletal remains is almost as difficult as estimation of age from living physiognomy. Accuracy and certainty of age from skeletal age decreases with increase in age of an individual, living or dead. Forensic anthropologists have deviced following measures for determining age through different stages of development.

1. *Neonate Period*

This period extends from birth up to the eruption of deciduous dentition. This stage indicates a lack of fusion of many skeletal elements, like neural arches of the vertebrae, epiphysis, halves of the frontal bone, segments of the innominate, etc. The crypts of the unerupted teeth are apparent in both jaws. It is extremely difficult to estimate age in such a young skeleton with precision. However, crown-heel or crown-rump length may indirectly help in a rough estimation of age (Oliver and Pineau, 1957). Oliver (1969) has provided following values for estimating age between 5 and 10 lunar months on the basis of foetal stature.

Foetal Stature (cm)	*Age in Lunar Months*
23.80	5 months
30.69	6 months
36.52	7 months
41.58	8 months
46.03	9 months
50.02	10 months

Johnston (1962) on the basis of growth in long bones provided mean lengths of the six long bones from foetal stage to 5 years on the basis of Kentucky skeletal population of Indian Knoll (Table 3) and suggested that the age of an individual could be assessed through this method.

2. *Infancy and Early Childhood Period*

A good number of features pertaining to skeletal immaturity obscrved during foetal period continue to persist during infancy and early childhood. During this period the halves of the frontal bone usually fuse into a single bone. An important marker for this age is the eruption of milk dentition which serves as a reliable measure of age. Besides dentition, the appearance of ossification centres aid determination of age during childhood (early and late) and adolescent periods. Krogman (1962) has specified about appearance of various ossification centres between 5 and 15 years (Table 4).

Using these as a reference age of skeletal material can be assessed depending upon the availability of the bones up to 15 years of age as a supplement to the dental age.

TABLE 3

Assessment of Age Through Length of Long Bones

Estimated Age in years	Long Bone Lengths (mm)											
	Humerus		Radius		Ulna		Femur		Tibia		Fibula	
	$\bar{X}$	S.D.	$\bar{X}$	S.D.	$\bar{X}$	S.D.	$\bar{X}$	S.D.	$\bar{X}$	S.D.	$\bar{X}$	S.D.
Foetal	56.78	6.26	47.20	5.42	54.80	4.12	61.86	6.33	55.50	7.54	50.00	—
Newborn-0.5	67.66	5.94	55.05	4.24	63.70	4.74	78.84	7.23	69.28	6.33	65.38	5.19
0.5-1.5	93.14	12.11	73.96	8.36	82,86	9.00	115.63	18.34	96.87	14.47	92.44	13.79
1.5-2.5	113.57	5.66	91.33	4.42	99.20	1.94	148.13	10.76	120.57	5.45	113.80	7.44
2.5-3.5	125.64	6.86	97.86	6.47	108.00	5.76	166.73	9.99	138.20	8.54	134.17	10.39
3.5-4.5	136.78	5.56	108.50	2.28	120.63	4.24	183.82	9.20	154.30	8.10	144.71	11.32
4.5-5.5	154.67	5.42	120.00	2.76	132,75	3.42	213.67	4.52	178.43	4.53	171.67	4.52

TABLE 4

Appearance of Ossification Centres after 5 years of Age

S. No.	Ossification centres	Male	Female
1.	Humerus : medial epicondyle	5.2 yrs	—
2.	Ulna : distal	5.6 yrs	—
3.	Calcaneal epiphysis	6.2 yrs	—
4.	Talar epiphysis	8.0 yrs	6.10 yrs
5.	Humerus : trochlea	8.4 yrs	7.2 yrs
6.	Olecranon	8.8 yrs	6.8 yrs
7.	Femur : lesser trochanter	9.4 yrs	7.7 yrs
8.	Pisiform	9.10 yrs	7.1 yrs
9.	Sesamoid	10.4 yrs	8.2 yrs
10.	Humerus : lateral condyle	10.5 yrs	8.3 yrs
11.	Tibial tubercle	10.10 yrs	9.0 yrs
12.	Metatarsal V : Proximal	11.0 yrs	8.7 yrs
13.	Rib I, tubercle	13.3 yrs	10.0 yrs
14.	Ilium ; anterior superior spine	13.4 yrs	9.3 yrs
15.	Thoracic vertebra I : transverse process	13.4 yrs	11.4 yrs
16.	Acromion	13.5 yrs	11.4 yrs
17.	Iliac crest	13.5 yrs	12.0 yrs
18.	Coracoid angle	13.10 yrs	11.3 yrs
19.	Ischial tuberosity	15.00 yrs	13.2 yrs
20.	Clavicle, medial	15.0+yrs	14.6 yrs

3. *Assessment of age Through Vertebral Ossification*

Before considering eruption of permanent teeth for assessing skeletal age, one may consider the ossification sites of the vertebrae for this purpose. Around the age of three years, the second cervical vertebra (the axis) consists of four pieces, viz. the two lateral portions that constitute the arch, the body, and the dens. The portions of the arch unite posteriorly at the same time when the deciduous dentition is completed. This is followed by the onset of fusion in the arches and the bodies of the lowest lumbar vertebrae.

At six years, when the first molar erupts, there begins the fusion of the other parts of the anterior portion of axis vertebra. This is followed by the posterior fusion of the two halves of the arch of the first cervical (atlas) vertebra. At around the same age the squamous and lateral parts of the occipital bone begin to join medially. However, these developments are highly variable as far as age is concerned, but in the absence of other skeletal parts a rough idea about the age can be given by observing the vertebral ossification.

4. *Late Childhood*

The initiation of late childhood is marked by the appearance of the first permanent tooth (Fig. 18). The dentition exhibits a combination of deciduous and permanent teeth for a certain number of years to come. The standards propounded by Schour and Massler (1940) are still considered to be the best estimates for determining dental age. They provided the following sequence of dental eruption during the late childhood period.

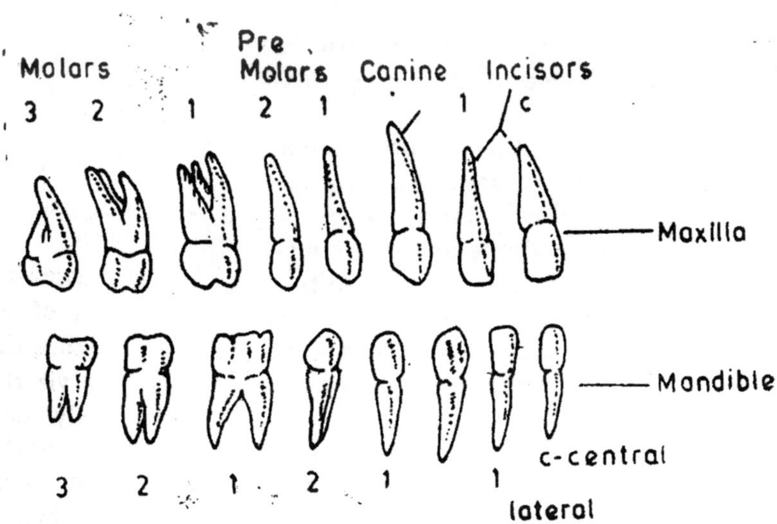

Fig 18 : Human Dentition

A. Deciduous Dentition

Event	*Age*
1. Beginning eruption of central upper incisors and all lower incisors.	: 6 months (±2)
2. Eruption of upper lateral incisors, completion of incisor set.	: 9 months (±3)
3. Eruption of lower molar (premolar).	: 12 months (±3)
4. Eruption of upper molar (premolar), beginning eruption of canines and second molar.	: 18 months (±3)
5. Complete eruption of all teeth except second molars.	: 24 months (±6)
6. Completion of deciduous dentition.	: 36 months (±6)

B. Mixed Dentition

1. Beginning eruption of first permanent molar. All deciduous teeth are retained at this age.	: 6 yrs (±9 months)
2. Loss of upper central deciduous incisors and all lower incisors. Beginning eruption of central upper permanent incisors and all lower incisors with the centrals in more advanced state of eruption than the laterals. Completion of first permanent molar eruption.	: 7 yrs (±9 months)
3. Beginning eruption of upper lateral permanent incisors. Loss of deciduous upper lateral incisors.	: 8 yrs (±9 months)
4. Completion of eruption of permanent incisors. At this age dentition consists of the permanent incisor set and permanent first molars plus deciduous canines and molars (premolars).	: 9 yrs (±9 months)
5. Beginning eruption of upper and lower first premolars and of lower canine. The deciduous molars (premolars) and lower canines are lost.	: 10 yrs (± 9 month)

C. Permanent Dentition

1. All deciduous teeth have been shed. Beginning eruption of upper canines and all second premolars. : 11 yrs (± 9 months)
2. Completion of all permanent dentition medial to (upto) first molar. Beginning eruption of second molar. : 12 yrs (± 6 months)
3. Completed eruption of second molars. : 15 yrs (± 6 months)
4. Eruption of third molar. Completing the permanent dentition. In certain cases the third molar may never appear. : 21 yrs*

*This age is quite variable and may fluctuate between 17 and 25 years.

The sequence of eruption of deciduous and permanent teeth is often referred to by the forensic anthropologist to evaluate age of skeletal material as well as living persons in case such a need arises. Kerley (1973) is of the opinion that it is possible to estimate age fairly close to the actual age by examining certain features of the teeth, but by the forensic dentists alone as it involves highly specialised techniques.

5. *Adolescence Phase*

The adolescence phase is marked by cessation over a period of time of length increase of most long bones, signalled by the fusion of the bony epiphysis of the bone to the shaft (diaphysis). The epiphyseal union occurs with quite a regularity to serve as an age marker. Each epiphysis fuses with the bone shaft at a particular age. The entire process of fusion from the first epiphysical union to the last extends over many years, but by 25 years it is completely fused. Mckern and Stewart (1957) have defined five stages of epiphyseal union as (1) unobservable (2) beginning, (3) active, (4) recent, and (5) complete union. The age distribution for epiphyseal union for long bones provided by them follows as under (Table-5).

TABLE 5

Distribution of age for Epiphyseal Union for Long Bones

Sl. No.	Bone	Beginning	Complete fusion
1.	Humerus, proximal	17—20 yrs	24 yrs
2.	Radius, distal	17 –18 yrs	23 yrs
3.	Ulna, distal	17—20 yrs	23 yrs
4.	Femur, distal	17—18 yrs	22 yrs
5.	Tibia, proximal	17—18 yrs	23 yrs
6.	Fibula, proximal	17—18 yrs	22 yrs
7.	Radius, proximal	—	19 yrs
8.	Ulna, proximal	—	19 yrs
9.	Femur, proximal	—	20 yrs
10.	Tibia, distal	—	20 yrs
11.	Fibula distal	—	20 yrs
12	Iliac crest, epiphysis	17—21 yrs	23—25 yrs
13.	Clavicle, medial	18—25 yrs	31 yrs
14.	Closure of Basilar suture	17—18 yrs	20—21 yrs

On the basis of the beginning and complete fusion of these epiphyseal unions and closure of the basilar suture, age can be assessed after a careful examination of these skeletal parts.

6. *Young Adult*

During this phase aging begins to turn from details of development to degeneration. Earlier, cranial suture closure was considered as an important age determining criteria for adults but the works of Mckern and Stewart (1957) have diminished their potentiality due to the irregular patterns observed which does not indicate or support a reliable terminal age of closure within the ages represented. They suggested that the closure of cranial sutures is erratic at least up to around 45 years. With an exception of basilar suture which is completely fused at the age of 21, which is a reliable indicator of the attainment of at least the age of 21 years, if fusion has occurred.

It has also been observed that more reliable and accurate age estimates can be arrived at by studying the combined maturational activity of a small number of critical growth areas. Age status of a skeleton can be estimated from the sum of scores for the epiphyseal activity of the following bone areas :

1. Medial end of clavicle,
2. Iliac crest,
3. Distal end of femur,
4. Head of femur,
5. Head of humerus,
6. Medial epicondyle of humerus,
7. Distal end of radius,
8. Lateral joints of sacrum,
9. 3-4 joints of sacrum.

Pubic symphysis is formed by the meeting of the right and the left innominate bones at the mid-line in front. This region provides the best estimation of age among young adults up to the age of 45 years. Assessment of age is based on the comparison of the face of pubic symphysis with standard casts of the symphysis known to be characteristic of certain ages. This method of age assessment is more reliable for males than females because of less regular changes and more rapid degeneration in females due to child birth.

McKern and Stewart (1957) modified the earlier methods of Todd (1920) and Brooks (1955) by examining the three components of pubic symphysis, i.e. Dorsal Plateau, Ventral Rampart and Symphyseal Rim, into five stages of development.

1. Dorsal Plateau

0. Dorsal margin absent.
1. Slight margin formation appears in the middle third of dorsal border.
2. Dorsal margin extends along the entire dorsal border.
3. Filling in of grooves and resorption of ridges to form a beginning plateau in the middle third of the dorsal demaiface.

4. The Plateau, still exhibiting vestiges of billowing, extends over the dorsal demiface.
5. Billowing disappears completely and the surface of the entire demiface becomes flat and slightly granulated.

2. **Ventral Rampart**
   0. Ventral beveling absent.
   1. Ventral beveling present at superior extremity of ventral border.
   2. Bevel extends inferiorly along ventral border.
   3. Ventral rampart begins by means of bony extensions from either or both extremities.
   4. Rampart extensive but gaps still evident along the earlier ventral border, most evident in the upper two-thirds.
   5. Rampart complete.

3. **Symphyseal Rim**
   0. Rim absent.
   1. Partial dorsal rim present, usually, at the superior end of the dorsal margin. It is round and smooth in texture and elevated above the symphyseal surface.
   2. Dorsal rim complete and ventral rim beginning to form. No particular beginning site.
   3. Rim complete. Enclosed symphyseal surface finely grained in texture and irregular in appearance.
   4. Rim begins to break down. Face becomes smooth and flat and the rim no longer round but sharply defined. Some evidence of lipping on the ventral edge.
   5. Further break down of the rim, along the superior ventral edge, with rarefaction of the symphyseal face. Also disintigration and erratic ossification along the ventral rim.

All these components progress slowly with increase in age through the five stages. In order to estimate age, each component is scored according to its development separately to determine the grade in which it falls. After obtaining grades of all the three components the grade scores are added together, with the resultant number, one enters a table to the age and standard deviation appropriate to that score (Table 6). For example, if the scores produced for the three components are I=4, II=3 and III=4, the resultant score, 10, would be sought in the following table. Score 10 indicates a mean age of 26.05 years with a standard deviation of 1.87, which is indicative of a likelihood that the correct age is within ±3.74 years. The observed range in ages for this score is 23 to 28 years.

TABLE 6

Estimated Age (to be used with casts) of male Pubic Symphysis

Score	Mean age (yrs)	S.D.	Age-range
0	17.29	0.49	—17
1-2	19.04	0.79	17-20
3	19.79	0.85	18-21
4-5	20.24	1.13	18-23
6-7	22.42	0.99	20-24
8-9	22.14	1.93	22-28
10	26.05	1.87	23-28
11-13	29.18	3.33	23-39
14	35.84	3.89	29+
15	41.00	6.22	36+

Gilbert and McKern (1973) using the method of McKern and Stewart (1957) devised a method for aging female skeletons using the pubic symphysis. They considered three components of the pubic symphysis and specified following stages in these components for assessing age.

Component-I

0. Ridges and furrows very distinct and billowed, dorsal margins undefined.
1. Ridges begin to flatten, furrows fill on, and a flat dorsal margin begins in middle-third of demiface.
2. Dorsal demiface streads ventrally, becomes wider as flattening continues, dorsal margin extends superiorly and inferiorly.

3. Dorsal demiface is quite smooth, margin may be narrow or indistinct from face.
4. Demiface becomes complete and unbroken, it is very broad and fine grained, may exhibit billowing.
5. Demiface becomes pitted and irregular through rarefaction.

Component-II

0. Ridges and furrows very distinct, the entire demiface is beveled up toward the dorsal demiface.
1. Beginning inferiorly, the furrows of the ventral demiface begin to fill in, forming an expanding beveled rampart, the lateral edge of which is distinct, curved line extending the length of the symphysis.
2. Fill in of furrows and expansion of demiface continues from both superior and inferior ends, rampart spreads laterally along its ventral edge.
3. All but above one-third of the ventral demiface is filled in with fine grained bone.
4. The ventral rampart presents a broad, complete fine grained surface from the pubic crest to the inferior ramus.
5. Ventral rampart may begin to break down assuming a very pitted and perhaps cancellous appearance through rarefaction.

Component-III

0. The rim is absent.
1. The rim begins in the middle third of the dorsal face.
2. The dorsal part of the symphyseal rim is complete.
3. The rim extends from the superior and inferior ends of the symphysis until all but above one-third of the ventral aspect is complete.
4. The symphyseal is complete.
5. The ventral margin of the dorsal demiface may breakdown so that gaps appear in the rim, or it may round off so that there is no longer a clear dividing line between the dorsal demiface and the ventral rampart.

In order to estimate age of female skeletons, each component is scored separately according to its development, in a similar manner as observed in case of male skeleton, to determine the grade into which it falls. The added grade score in the form of a resultant number is checked from the following age estimation table for females (Table 7).

TABLE 7

Estimated Age (to be used with casts) of female Pubic Symphysis

Score	Mean Age (yrs)	S.D.	Age-range
0	16.00	2.82	14-18
1	19.80	2.62	13-24
2	20.15	2.19	16-25
3	21.50	3.10	18-25
4-5	26.00	2.61	22-29
6	29.62	4.43	25-36
7-8	32.00	4.55	23-39
9	33.00	7.75	22-40
10-11	36.90	4.94	30-47
12	39.00	6.09	32-52
13	47.75	3.59	44-54
14-15	55.71	3.24	52-59

This method for aging female pubic symphysis has much wider standard deviation than that used for males and, therefore, less likelihood of achieving greater accuracy in estimated age for female skeletons. The cause for the sexual difference is attributed to child birth trauma to the pubic symphysis in females (Gilbert, 1973).

7. *Older Adults*

Determination of age beyond 45 years is most difficult due to the tendency towards degeneration of teeth and skeleton. By this age arthritis has almost appeared in the vertebrae, but its severity is not a reliable indicator of age, since it varies with individual. Around this age the teeth generally exhibit wear facets. The apices of the cusps may only be blunted or the crown may be worn to the gum line. However, no precise method of age estimation by gross examination is known for older adult skeletons excepting microscopic inspection of thin sections of adult bone which will provide a precise estimation of age in this age group. Kerley (1965) suggested bone section examination for the following :

1. the number of osteones,
2. the number of fragments of old osteones,
3. the percentage of circumferential lamellar bone,
4. the number of non haversian canals.

It has been observed that of these four items, 1 and 2 increase with increasing age while 3 and 4 decrease, disappearing altogether around fifty-five years of age. Schranz (1959) suggested a method for age determination based on age-changes observed in the trabeculae of the proximal humerus and combined that with the observations of the earlier researchers (Walholz, 1894 ; Beuno, 1934 ; Hansen, 1954) to arrive at the following observations :

15-16 years : The metaphysis is cartilaginous.

17-18 years : Union is beginning between diaphysis and epiphysis. The internal structure of the diaphysis is arch like.

19-20 years : Union of the epiphysis and the diaphysis is nearly complete. Internally, the structure of the epiphysis is arranged radially while that of the diaphysis remain arched.

21-22 years : Union of the two parts is complete. The internal structure remains the same.

23-25 years : The internal structure of the epiphysis is less radial. The diaphyseal structure remains arched the medullary cavity is widely separated from the surgical neck.

26-30 years : The arrangement of the trabeculae in the epiphysis is becoming less radial, that of the diaphysis remains arched. The medullary cavity

	approaches, but has not yet reached the surgical neck of the bone.
31-40 years :	The internal structure of the epiphysis is no longer radial, while that of the diaphysis has become more columnar. The medullary cavity approaches the surgical neck.
41-50 years :	The columnar structure of the diaphysis is discontinuous. The cone of the medullary cavity reaches the surgical neck with occasional lacunae in the epiphyseal structure of the epiphyseal line.
51-60 years :	The lacunae become more common and pea-size cavities appear in the trabeculae of the epiphysis.
61-74 years :	The Cortex of the bone is thin, and externally it is roughened. The characteristic features of the structure of diaphysis disappear. The cavity of the medulla reaches the epiphyseal line. Bean sized or larger lacunae appear on the trabeculae of the epiphysis.
74+ years :	The tuberculum majus is much less prominent and little spongy tissue remains in the medullary cavity.

Schranz further suggests that the X-ray pictures are not useful for age estimation and it is necessary to see the bone lengthwise for visual examination. It is also necessary to know the sex of the individual from whom the bone came as the age dependent changes, during growth, occur at different rates for both the sexes. Generally speaking, females are nearly two years advanced over males at puberty, five years at maturity and seven to ten years in old age.

Cranial features have also been used for assessing age of the skeletal material in question. According to Terry (1942) the sphenoid and mastoid fontanelles close soon after birth while occipital and frontal fontanelees close during first year and second year respectively. The mandibular symphysis unites completely in second year. The metopic suture often closes in second year. Similarly, in atlas vertebra the posterior union occurs in third year and anterior in sixth year. The different parts of the axis vertebra exhibit occurrence of union between third and fourth year. The squamous and lateral parts of occipital bone unites in fifth year while its lateral and basilar parts unite by seventh year. According to McKern and Stewart (1957) the final age for union of primary elements of the innominate in males is 17 years while the spheno-occipital synchondrosis is closed by 21 years of age.

Pommeral (1869), Ribbe (1885), Dwight (1890) and Frederic (1906) reported on the aspect of age determination from cranial suture closure. Later Todd and Lyon (1924;1925) provided a detailed account regarding commencement and termination of following sutures—sagittal, sphenofrontal-orbital, sphenofrontal-temporal, coronal, lambdoid, masto-occipital, spheno-parietal, spheno-temporal,parieto-mastoid and squamous for estimation of age between 20 and 80 years as shown in Table-8.

In comparison to the epiphyseal development and examination of cranial sutures, dental development shows less variability (Lewis and Garn, 1960), and offers a more relaible means of age estimation in skeleton through the first 13 years of post natal life. Tooth emergence is the traditional way of translating dental development into chronological age. Dentists have long known, in a general way, the sequence of developmental events that the teeth undergo in the depths of the jaw.

Physical anthropologists have used wear of occlusal surface as a criterion of aging. Gustavson (1950 ; 1966) used tooth sections for this purpose and later Helfman and Bada (1976) attempted the same based on racemization of aspertic acid in dentine but in both these methods the specimen must be sacrificed for the purpose of age estimation.

It may be emphasised here that while dealing with foetal and immature postnatal skeletons great care of exhumation must be observed not only in the process of recovery but also in the idea regarding search of separate bony elements, because the presence of epiphysis will yield a much more accurate estimate of age at the time of death. On the other hand while dealing

TABLE 8

Probable Ages of Cranial Suture closure among White and Negro males

Suture	Endocranial				Ectocranial			
	White male		Negro male		White male		Negro male	
	C (yrs)	T (yrs)	C (yrs)	T (yrs)	C (yrs)	T (yrs)	C (yrs)	T (yrs)
1. Sagittal	22	35	21	31	20	29	20	32
2. Spheno-frontal-orbital	22	64	20	44	28	46	21	35
3. Spheno frontal-temporal	22	65	23	44	28	38	25	46
4. Coronal 1 & 2	24	38	24	38	26	29	23	32
5. Coronal 3	26	41	25	44	28	50	25	35
6. Lambdoid 1 & 2	26	42	23	46	26	30	23	31
7. Lambdoid 3	26	47	27	46	26	31 ?	22	31 ?
8. Masto-occipital	26	72	17	30	26	33	26	31
9. Spheno-parietal	29	65	23	49	28	38	28	46
10. Spheno-temporal-2	30	67	40	51	36	65 ?	50 ?	P.N.C
11. Spheno-tempotal-1	31	64	40	41	37	65 ?	50 ?	P.N.C
12. Masto-occipital	30	81	25	46	28	32	27	31
13. Parieto-mastoid	37	81	33	51	39	64 ?	50 ?	P.N.C
14. Squamous posterior	37	81	40	49	38	65 ?	50 ?	P.N.C
15. Squamous anterior	37	81	40	49	38	65 ?	50 ?	P.N.C

C—Commencement, T—Termination,
P.N.C.—Probably never closes.

with skeletons between 5 and 19 years different age tables should be used for males and females in the recognition of the fact that the latter are advanced in maturation process. Thus, depending upon the completeness of the recovered postnatal immature skeletons an accuracy of ± one year could be achieved. In case of adult skeleton the pubic symphysis is probably the best single criterion of assessing age in the skeleton. But in correlation with other parts of the skeleton it should facilitate aging within an accuracy of ± 2.5 years.

B. Age Changes in Scapula

According to Graves (1922) age changes attributed to ossification are equally discernible in scapulae, whether fixed (embalmed) or unfixed. If the bones have been macerated without previous fixation, the picture of the changes in superficial and deep vascularity is altered, but the other features incident to an atrophic process are readily discernible in fixed and unfixed bones. The following characteristics may be observed to assess the age changes due to ossification after maturity.

1. Lipping of the circumferential margin of the glenoid fossa: usually begins at the depression located at the junction of the upper and middle thirds of the ventral margin (begins at 30-35 years). The order of progression is usually ventral, inferior, dorsal and superior margins.
2. Lipping of the clavicular facet : seldom uniform, but may involve entire margin (begins at 35-40 years).
3. Appearance of a facet in the underside of the acromial process : often prolongs acromion tip from 2 to 8 mm or more (beigns at 35 to 40 or 40 to 45 years).
4. Increasing demarcation of the triangular area at the base (vertebral margin) of the scapular spine : Begins at 50 years or over.
5. Appearance of cristae scapulae (50 years or over) : although variable in number and development, they tend to become broader at their bases, more prominent and their apices more roughened with advancing age.

Following characteristics may be observed to assess age changes due to an atrophic process after maturity.

1. Surface vascularity : seen as a number of fine delicate lines (below 25 years of age). Diminish in visibility and finally disappear as age advances. It may vary with fixation of bone.
2. Deep vascularity : seen as similar lines, but now by transillumination only (25-30 years). They tend to diminish with age but never wholly disappear.
3. Atrophic spots : localized, discrete, or coalescing areas of bone atrophynated by transillumination, especially in the infraspinous fossa (begins at 45 years). Patchiness in vascularity is probably a forerunner of these spots.
4. Buckling and pleating of the infraspinous area : (early thirties and after) leading to actual distortion (40 years and over). These phenomena appear to depend upon altered vascularity leading to irregular bone absorption (atrophy) especially of the cancellous tissue.

C. Assessment of Age from the Bones of Hand

Human hand is divided into three main parts, viz. wrist, palm and fingers (Fig. 19). The skeleton of wrist consists of eight carpal bones, which belong to the category of irregular bones. These eight carpals are arranged in two rows with four bones in each. The first (proximal) row consists of the following bones :

1. Scaphoid or Navicular,
2. Lunate,
3. Triquetral, and
4. Pisiform.

The second (distal) row consists of the following four bones :

1. Trapezium,
2. Trapezoid,
3. Capitate, and
4. Hamate.

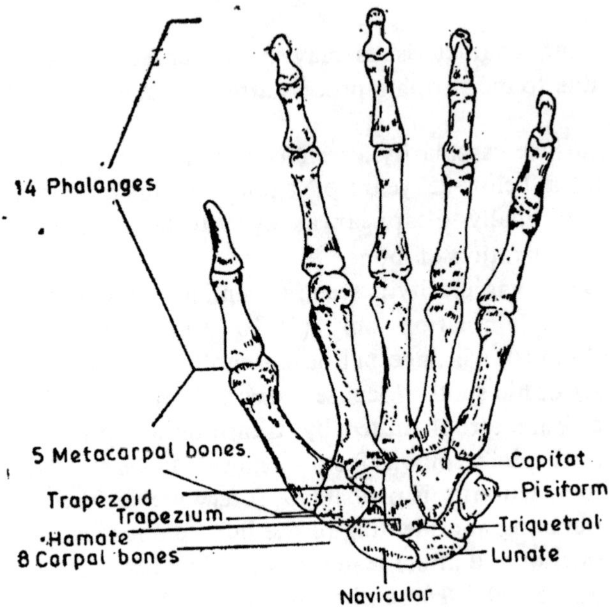

Fig. 19 : Posterior view of Human hand

The skeleton of palm consists of five cylindrical bones which are known as metacarpals. These metacarpals belong to the short bone category and are articulated with the carpus proximally and with the first or proximal row of phalanges distally. All the metacarpals possess a shaft and two extremities.

Finally, the skeleton of fingers consists of 14 phalanges in each hand in three rows for all fingers except thumb where they are arranged in two rows only. The first or proximal row contains five phalanges. The second or middle row contains four phalanges, and the third or terminal row again contains five phalanges. All the 14 phalanges belong to short bone category and they possess a shaft and two extremities.

The entire carpus is cartilaginous at birth and each bone is ossified from a single ossification centre. Except the pisiform, all the carpal bones have six surfaces. At birth the bones of the hand consists of five metacarpals and fourteen phalanges. Epiphyses are not present and none of the carpal bones has begun to ossify.

At the age of one year, the ossification of the capitate and hamate begin in males and the epiphyses are still not present. The females, on the other hand, exhibit ossification of not only capitate and hamate but also of the distal epiphysis of the radius, the epiphyses of the second and third metacarpals and the proximal phalanges of the second, third and fourth fingers, through the recently formed ossification centres.

The males exhibit the epiphysis for the radius which is nearly three-fourths as wide as the distal end of the shaft at the age of five years. There is no epiphysis for the ulna at this age but all the carpals, excepting scaphoid and trapezoid, have ossified. The epiphysis of the first metacarpal is more than half as wide as its metaphysis. The epiphyses of the other metacarpals and proximal phalanges have enlarged while that of the middle and distal phalanges have ossified.

The carpals have ossified by five years among females but there is still no epiphysis on the distal end of the radius. All the epiphyses of the metacarpals and phalanges are ossified and have expanded in size. The epiphyses of the middle phalanges of the second, third and fourth fingers are shaping to the contour of the trochlear surfaces of the proximal phalanges, while the distal phalanges of the third, fourth and fifth fingers are, at five years, as broad as their shaft.

At ten year the epiphyses for the radius, ulna, metacarpals and phalanges are ossified among males. The epiphyses of the phalanges are nearly as broad as their shafts while those of the distal phalanges of the second to fifth fingers are slightly broader than their respective shafts. (Greulich and Pyle, 1959).

Females at this age, on the other hand, exhibit an advanced ossification of all epiphyses than the males. The styloid process of the ulnar epiphysis exhibits its formation. The epiphyses of the distal phalanges have begun to cap their shafts.

At the age of 15 the epiphysis of the radius has caped its shaft while that of the ulna is as wide as its shaft among males. In the case of females the epiphyses of radius and ulna have begun to fuse with their respective shafts with ulna exhibiting advancement in the process of fusion over radius.

The carpals, at this age, have nearly attained their early adult shape and the fusion of the epiphyses of all the distal phalanges is advancing at a high speed in males. Females, on the other hand, exhibit near complete fusion in all the carpal epiphyses.

The progression of fusion follows a disto-proximal mode, i. e. fusion is completed first in the distal phalange and is followed by the proximal one. It occurs last in the middle phalanges of the second, third, fourth and fifth fingers.

The fusion is completed by 17 years in females and by 19 in males. In order to estimate age through the skeleton of hand it is necessary to observe the proper development and the extent of ossification that has taken place in various bones (carpals, metacarpals and phalanges) of the hand.

Differentiation between the Short Bones of the Hand and Foot

The metacarpals and metatarsals and the phalanges of both may lead to some confusion with regard to their identification as their number is exactly alike.

In order to differentiate between metacarpals of hand and metatarsals of foot following points should be considered (Bass, 1971) :

1. The metatarsals are longer and their shafts are thinner than that of the metacarpals, excepting the first one.
2. The articular surfaces on the heads of the metatarsals are restricted laterally and are well-marked anteriorly-posteriorly, thus it gives an appearance of having a groove causing double expansion of the head.
3. The grooves between the articular facets on the proximal margin of the metatarsals are highly pronounced, deeper and more rugged than the ones on the metacarpals.

Differentiation between metacarpals and metatarsals can be made considering these points while examining the skeletal material in question.

The phalanges of the hand (fingers) and foot (toes) are equal in number, i.e. 14 in both the hand and the foot. Following points should be considered to differentiate them :

1. All the phalanges of the toes are smaller and more rudimentary than the corresponding ones of the fingers excepting the two phalanges of the big toe which are larger in size than the two phalanges of the thumb.
2. The phalanges of the fingers are flat on the palmar surface and rounded on the dorsal surface.
3. The shaft is narrow and compressed in the phalanges of the toes in comparison to the phalanges of the fingers, and the the bone are not as long as in the fingers.

However, the nutrient foramina, which are extremely difficult to locate in these bones, extend toward the distal end in both the fingers and toes. Considering these aspects, it is possible to discriminate between the phalanges of the fingers and toes in skeletal material under examination.

D. Determination of Age from a Single Tooth

Gustafson (1950) reported about the changes that occur in teeth with increasing age and succeeded in evolving a method for estimating age with some accuracy. He examined longitudinal ground section of the tooth by naked eye as well as under microscope for evidence of attrition, periodontosis secondary tidenn, cementum apposition, root resorption and root transparency(Fig. 20). The section is prepared by grinding the tooth from two sides towards the centre until a thin film, 0.25 mm thickness, remains. This method is only applicable to permanent teeth. Decalcified sections and molars are not suitable for this observation.

Attrition : Takes place with the wearing down of incisal or occlusal surfaces due to mastication, and can be observed both macroscopically and microscopically.

Periodontosis : Pertains to loosening of the tooth or continuous eruption and is characterised by changes in the attachment of the tooth. The gum margin becomes retracted. This can also be seen macroscopically and microscopically.

Secondary Dentin : It may form within the pulp cavity partly as a result of aging and partly as a reaction to pathological conditions such as caries and periodontosis. This change is observed only through microscopy.

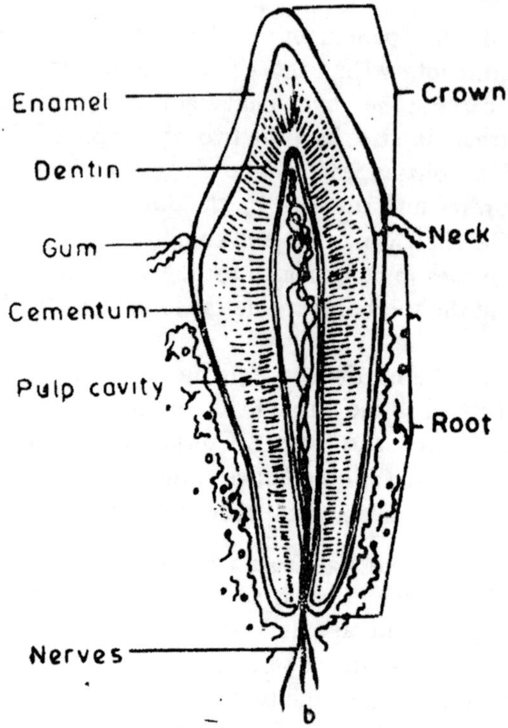

Fig. 20 : Longitudinal Section of a Human Tooth

Cementum Apposition : It pertains to the apposition of cementum at and around the tooth and can be observed only in microscopic sections.

Root resorption : This involves both cementum and dentin and is best observed in microscopic section.

Root transparency : The transparency of the apical parts of the root is best appreciated on ground section but is also visible at times on an unprepared tooth. The transparency should be observed before it is mounted, since the mounting medium is likely to percolate into the dentinal tubules which variates the root transparency (Johnson, 1971).

Ranking of age changes : Each change is ranked arbitrarily and assigned numerical values like 0, 1, 2, 3, and so on depending upon the degree of structural changes.

Thus the different stages are ranked in the following manner to estimate age from a tooth.

Attrition is referred to as	A
No attrition is denoted as	A—0
Attrition lying within enamel as	A—1
Attrition reaching the dentin as	A—2
Attrition reaching pulp as	A—3
Periodontosis is referred to as	P
No periodontosis is denoted as	P—0
Periodontosis just begun as	P—1
Periodontosis has peneterated along the first 1/3 of the root as	P—2
Periodontosis has passed 2/3 of the root as	P—3
Secondary dentin is denoted as	S
No secondary dentin is visible as	S—0
It has just begun to form the upper part of pulp cavity as	S—1
Pulp cavity is half filled as	S—2
Pulp cavity is completely filled by secondary dentin as	S—3
Cementum apposition is referred to as	C
Normal layer of cementum is laid down as	C—0
A little greater layer of cementum than normal as	C—1
A great layer of cementum as	C—2
A heavy layer of cementum as	C—3
Root resorption is referred to as	R
No visible root resorption as	R—0
Resorption only on small isolated spots as	R—1
Greater loss of substance as	R—2
Major areas of cementum and dentin are affected as	R—3
Transparency in root is denoted as	T
Transparency not present as	T—0
Transparency is just noticeable as	T—1
It extends to apical 1/3 of the root as	T—2
It extends over the apical 2/3 of the root as	T—3

Point formula : The point value of each age change assessed as mentioned above are added in the following formula :

$A_n+P_n+S_n+C_n+R_n+T_n=\text{Points}$

It is observed that increasing age is associated to increasing point values. Gustafson used the point values of teeth of known age to evolve a regression equation and plotted regression line to represent relationship between age and point value.

In order to estimate age of an individual the point value for the tooth in question is entered on a chart, its crossing with the regression line is read, and the corresponding age read off from the graph.

Despite the obvious advantage of this method the major drawback is that a tooth has to be sacrificed.

CHAPTER 6

MORPHOLOGICAL VARIATIONS IN TEETH

Forensic odontology, according to Goldman (1982) is that branch of dentistry which deals with the proper handling and examination of dental evidence and the proper evaluation and presentation of dental findings in the interest of justice.

The main job of the forensic odontologist is to identify the unknown human remains in different stages of decomposition through an analysis of dentition of the deceased by recording dental anomalies, missing teeth and other peculiarities. These findings when compared with antemortem dental records and radiographs (wherever available) may lead to a positive identification (Standish and Stimson, 1977).

Following variations in tooth number and position are useful, at times, in identification process :

1. *Supernumerary teeth* : These are extra teeth that may occur in the incisors, canine, premolar or molar tooth groups. Supernumerary teeth may appear as replicas of the normal teeth or they may exhibit a shape that does not resemble any particular tooth. Their eruption is rare in the deciduous dentition as compared to the permanent one. Supernumerary teeth will occur bilaterally as a result of retention of deciduous teeth in the permanent (adult) dentition. The proper antemortem records, if maintained, pertaining to presence of

supernumerary teeth, may prove useful in establishing identity of a person.

2. *Rotation of teeth* : Generally the teeth are arranged in proper position in the dental arcade but occasionally a tooth may appear to be rotated up to 180°. Whenever a tooth has rotated, the normal distal surface may become lingual surface or vice versa. This situation provides an important clue for establishing identity of a person even in cases of mass disasters, provided that the antemortem dental records are available. The process of rotation is most commonly observed in the second premolars, however, other teeth can also undergo rotation (Fig. 21).

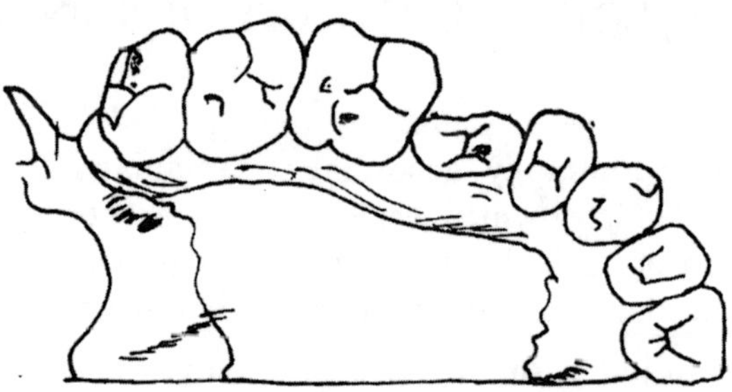

Fig. 21 : Rotated Second Maxillary Premolar

3. *Congenital absence of teeth* : In certain individuals one or more teeth, normally present in the dental arch, may be missing. The investigator must be careful not to confuse congenital absence of teeth with unerupted teeth. Detection of unerupted teeth is possible through radiography. However, those teeth that were originally present but lost before examination pose a problem. If the teeth were lost after death, the cavities for the roots will be present in the alveoli, but if a tooth was lost before death, the alveolus may have resorbed leaving no indication of the root cavity. However, the antemortem loss of tooth can be detected by the distorted and unequal appearance of the alveolus or through presence of wear facets on the appropriate surfaces of the adjacent teeth. Of all the teeth, the third molars are most frequently missing but any of the other teeth may be congenitally absent.

4. *Crowding of teeth* : It is a situation when one or more teeth are pushed out of their normal position as a result of

reduction in size of the mandible without a corresponding reduction in the size of the teeth. Crowding generally accompanies impacted third molars and rotated condition of teeth. Of all the teeth, the incisors are the most affected by crowding in permanent dentition while this problem is extremely rare in deciduous dentition, Antemortem dental record of such variations prove to be of great use in identification.

5. *Extra cusps* : These have been observed on both maxillary and mandibular molars. These are generally of two types, i.e. (1) protostylids, and (2) carabelli's cusps.

A *protostylid* is an extra cusp that appears on the anterior side of the buccal surface of the mandibular molars (Fig. 22). According to Dahlberg (1950) its appearance is rare in modern populations as it occurs in varying degree of prominence and is usually recorded as present or absent.

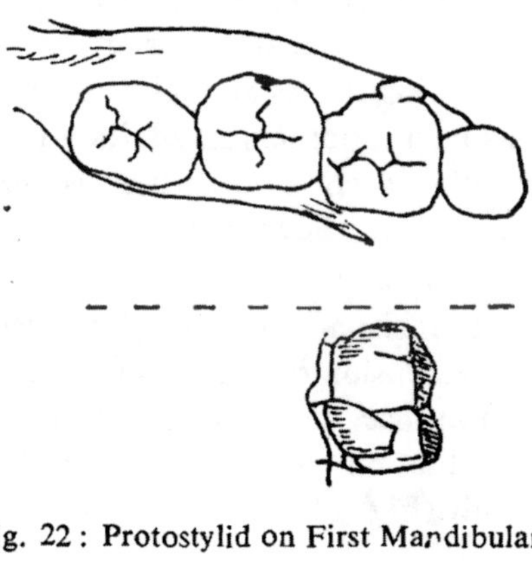

Fig. 22 : Protostylid on First Mandibular Molar

Carabelli's Cusp (tuberculum carabelli) consists of a tubercle present on the anterior part of the lingual surfaces of the maxillary molars. The extra cusp may occur in any form ranging from a pit (carabelli's pit) considered to be related to the cusp, to a well developed cusp. According to Karus (1959) Carabelli's cusp appears to be a recent evolutionary development that occurs in varying frequencies in different modern populations (Fig. 23). Presence of an additional cusp in the dentition provides an extra clue to a forensic odontologist for establishing identity of skeletal remains provided that the antemortem records are available.

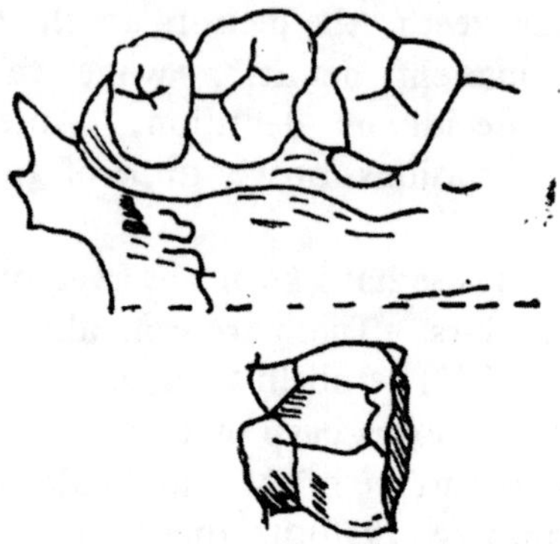

Fig. 23 : Carabelli's Cusp First Maxiilary Molar

6. *Shovel-shaped teeth* : Shovel-shaping of the incisors is one of the most commonly discussed genetic character. Morphologically it involves a lingual extension of the lateral borders of the incisors. Sometimes an incisor may exhibit a buccal extension of its lateral borders in addition to the lingual one. The incisor exhibiting such a condition is termed as a double shovel-shaped incisor. Such incisors are usually maxillary but this phenomenon may occur in the mandible as well.

Occasionally some incisors may display excessive pronouncement of lingual extension of the lateral borders that the tooth assumes the appearance of a distorted premolar or a barrel shape. This situation is observed generally on maxillary lateral incisors only (Fig. 24).

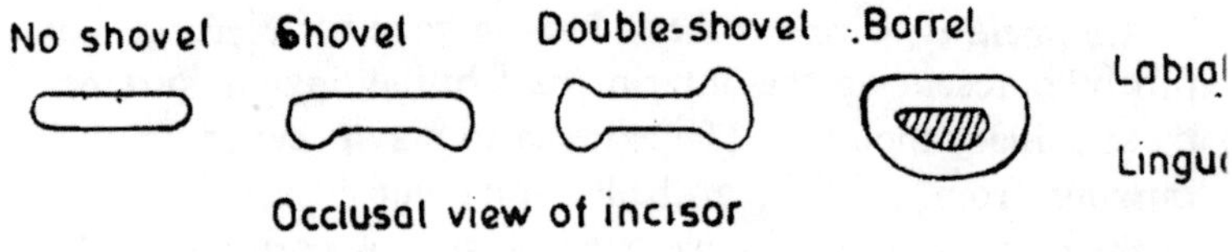

Fig. 24 : Shovel-Shaping of the Incisors

Shovel-shaping of any nature, i.e. single, double or barrel shaping, is a peculiar character that may serve as an important clue in establishing identity of skeletal remains.

7. *Peg-shaping* : Peg-shaping appears to be related to congenital absence of teeth and has been reported in almost all modern populations. It is related to the appearance of abnormally small third molar and lateral incisors in comparison to their normal size. The antemortem records of peg-shaping, if available, may prove to be an important evidence in establishing identity of skeletal remains.

8. *Tourodontism* : It is a character observed in those molars in which the pulp cavity is enlarged and the roots are reduced in size (Fig. 25). This condition has been found to occur occasionally in certain modern populations only. The occurrence of enlarged pulp cavity in a molar would be an important clue in the process of identification.

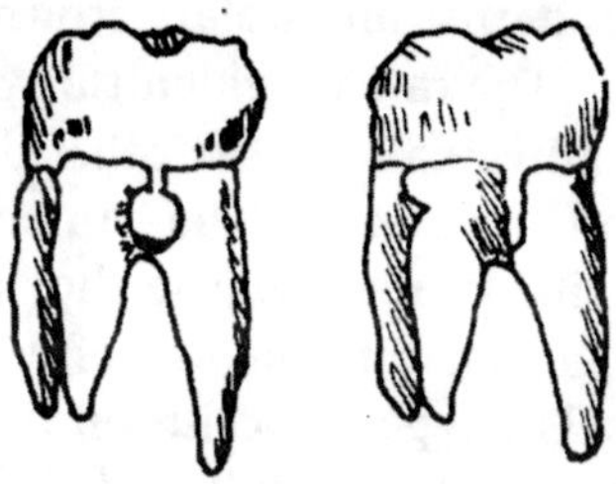

Fig. 25 : Taurodontism in Molar

9. *Extra or missing roots* : A tooth may occasionally exhibit an additional root or the absence of root in case of molars. Such an information may be useful in the process of identification.

10. *Enamel extensions and Pearl* : Sometimes an extension of the crown enamel is observed between the roots of molars and premolars. In certain cases this extension of enamel culminates in a cluster which is termed as enamel pearl. Enamel extension and pearl formation are unique characters and have been observed in many populations with variable frequency (Fig. 26).

11. *Occlusal wear or Attrition* : The mandibular and maxillary teeth continually rule against each other, during the process of mastication. This process of continuous rubbing

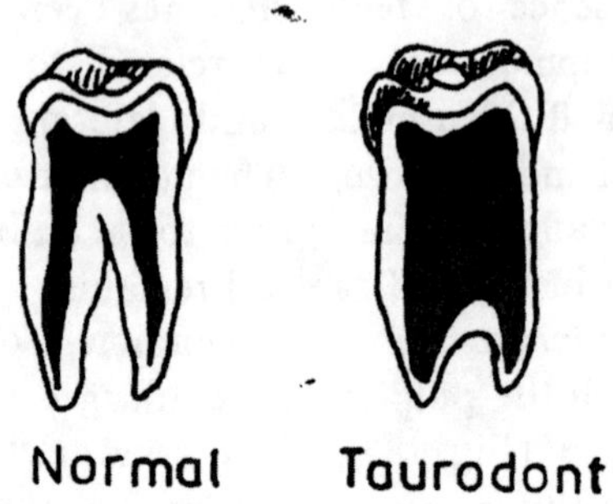

Fig. 26 : Enamel Pearl and Extension on Molars

eventually wear down the occlusal surfaces of the teeth and distort the cusp patterns on molar crowns by exposing the underlying dentine. The rate at which this process takes place varies from one individual to the other depending upon the diet of the person involved The antemortem records of occlusal wear, if available, may help in the process of identification as well as in estimating the age of a person.

12. *Occlusion* : The type of occlusion between the mandibular and maxillary teeth in adults is helpful in getting some idea regarding ethnicity (race) of a person. It has been observed (Bass, 1971) that Mongoloids frequently exhibit edge-to-edge occlusion of the teeth while Caucasoids largely display a slight overbite so that the maxillary incisors project more anteriarly than the mandibular ones. The underbites are rare types and may be found occasionally in any racial (ethnic) group (Fig. 27).

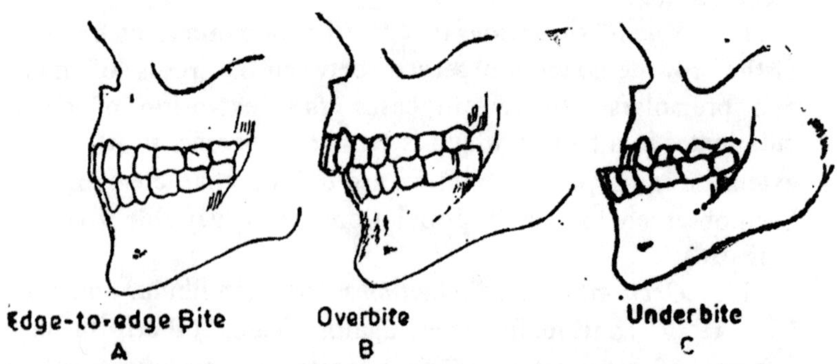

Fig. 27 : Types of Occlusion of Maxillary and Mandibular Teeth

13. *Artificial deformation* : Artificial deformation of teeth is by-and-large related to the cultural practices in different parts of the world. Romero (1958) classified seven types of dental mutilations prevalent in Mexico. Similar observations have also been reported from Africa, Australia, Egypt, Malaya and from different parts of the New World. Of all the teeth, incisors are the most commonly involved in dental, mutilations as they are the most visible from outside the mouth (Fig. 28).

Fig. 28 : Artificial Deformation by Grooves

Several American Indian tribes exhibit artificial interproximal grooving in the molar regions (Ubelaker et al., 1969). These grooves are created near the junction of the crown and the root of the concerned tooth. These grooves were probably produced in an attempt to relieve discomfort in the particular region caused due to decayed lesions, alveolar abscesses, or alveolar resorption due to periodontal disease. Such deformations may easily be overlooked but for a forensic expert they prove to be an important identification clue depending upon the availability of antemortem records.

14. *Dental caries* : It is that condition of the teeth in which the enamel or dentine is decalcified and the remaining organic material disintegrated. Dental caries usually develop in one or more regions of the tooth at the occlusal surface. The labial surface of the anterior teeth is usually the most affected by this disease (Fisher el. al. 1931). For the initiation of carious process the carbohydrates have been most often blamed as they provide a fermentable substrate which leads to the formation of acid on the surface of the teeth which subsequently decalcify the enamel.

15. *Periodontal disease* : This is an infection of the

alveolar bone and the soft tissues surrounding the teeth. This disease causes recession of the alveolar bone that results in loosening of the teeth and their eventual loss. This disease may be caused due to nutritional imbalance, calculus deposits and attrition.

The antemortem records, if available, for these pathological conditions may provide some positive clues for identification.

16. *Dental Enamel Hypoplasia* : It is a developmental defect in the enamel of the deciduous and permanent teeth. It results in structural changes observed as pits, transverse lines and grooves on the surface of the enamel. The most common variety of enamel hypoplasia involves a number of teeth in which formation of the enamel matrix occurs at the same time. This condition of teeth, if detected during the lifetime of an individual, can help in identifying a person.

DENTAL TERMINOLOGY

ALVEOLAR PROCESS : The process of the maxilla and mandible which holds the roots of the teeth.

ALVEOLUS : A cavity in the alveolar process of both the maxilla and mandible in which the root of the tooth is anchored.

ANGLE : The area of junction of two intersecting surfaces or borders.

APEX : The terminal end of the root.

BICUSPID : A tooth with two cusps, i.e. the pre molar.

BUCCAL : The side of the tooth adjacent to the cheek.

CEMENTUM : A bony tissue which covers the outer surface of the roots of the teeth.

CREST : A ridge bordering a bone.

CROWN : It is that part of the tooth which

		is situated above the gums and covered with enamel.
CUSP	:	A pronounced elevation on the crown surface of the tooth.
CUSPID	:	A tooth with one cusp, i.e. canine.
CUTTING EDGE	:	The edge formed by the junction of the labial and lingual surfaces of the incisors and canines.
DENTIN	:	The tissue which forms the main body of the tooth. It surrounds the pulp cavity and underlies the enamel of the crown and the cementum of the roots.
DISTAL	:	It is that surface of the tooth which lies against an adjoining tooth and faces away from the median line.
ENAMEL	:	The white hard tissue that covers the crown of the tooth.
FISSURE	:	A fault in the surface of the tooth caused by imperfect joining of the enamel of the different lobes.
FOSSA		A round or angular depression in the surface of the tooth.
GROOVE	:	A narrow depression between the main parts of the occlusal surfaces of the tooth.
INCISOR	:	A tooth with one cutting edge.
LABIAL	:	Toward the lips.
LABIAL SURFACE	:	The surface of the tooth adjacent to the lips. Only incisors and canines have labial surface.
LINGUAL	:	Toward the tongue.
MEDIAN LINE	:	The anteroposterior perpendicular central line of the body.
MESIAL	:	Toward the midline. The surfaces

of the tooth which lies against an adjoining tooth and faces toward the median line.

NECK : The portion of the tooth which forms the junction of the crown and root.

OCCLUSAL SURFACE : The surface of the premolars and molars that comes in contact with the teeth of the opposite jaw when the mouth is closed.

PITS : A Small pin-point depression in the enamel.

PULP : The soft tissue that fills the pulp chambers and root canals of the teeth and contains the nerves and blood vessels.

RIDGE : A long linear elevation on the surface of the tooth.

ROOT : It is that part of the tooth which lies below the crown and neck. It is enclosed in tooth socket and covered with cementum.

SULCUS : A long depression in the surface of the tooth between ridges and cusps.

TUBERCLE : A small rounded elevation on the surface of the tooth.

CHAPTER 7

RACIAL DIFFERENCES

Jones (1930-31) mentioned that non metric cranial traits are exceedingly helpful in determination of race. Krogman (1955) provides the descriptive morphology of the skull in three main human groups, i.e. Caucasoid (European), Negroid (African) and Mongoloid (Asiatic). He further subdivides Caucasoids into Nordic, Alpine and Mediterranean. Major differences observed by Krogman are as follows (Table 9) :

Though it is extremely difficult to opine after observing a single skull and classifying it as White, Negro or Mongoloid. However, Giles and Elliot (1960) used discriminant function analysis (D.F.A.) in 408 skulls of known race from Todd and Terry collections and successfully classified over 90 per cent of the sample.

Hrdlicka (1942) studied scapula in detail and commented that "the racial and group differences in both the descriptive features and the dimensions of the scapula are, on the whole, but moderate and do not in any case amount to safe criteria for distinguishing the groups. The basic proportions of the bone are throghout much alike." The differences that crop out are evidently mainly those due to stature, sex side and muscular variation or activity.

TABLE 9

Major Racial Differences in Cranial Traits of the Three Major Groups

Morphological Character	Caucasoid			Negroid	Mongoloid
	Nordic	Alpine	Mediterranean		
Cranial length	Long	Short	Long	Long	Long
Cranial breadth	Narrow	Broad	Narrow	Narrow	Broad
Cranial height	High	High	Moderately high	Low	Middle
Sagittal contour	Rounded	Arched	Rounded	Flat	Arched
Face breadth	Narrow	Wide	Narrow	Narrow	Very wide
Face height	High	High	Moderately high	Low	High
Orbital opening	Angular	Rounded	Angular	Rectangular	Rounded
Nasal opening	Narrow	Moderately wide	Narrow	Wide	Narrow
Lower nasal margin	Sharp	Sharp	Sharp	Troughed	Sharp
Facial profile	Straight	Straight	Straight	Downward Slant	Straight

Palate shape	Narrow	Moderately wide	Narrow	Wide	Modera-tely wide
General impression of the skull	Massive, Rugged, Elongated, Ovoid	Large, Moderately rugged Rounded	Small, Smooth, Elongated Pentagonoid, to ovoid	Massive, Smooth, Elongated. Constricted oval	Large, Smooth, Rounded

In general it may be stated here that the race differences in the skeleton are best known for American studies pertaining to Whites and Negroes on the basis of Todd and Terry collections.

Morphometric and morphological analysis could reveal the race of the skull in only 85 to 90 per cent cases while the accuracy is beyond 90 per cent through the use of discriminant function analysis (D.F.A.).

The lower jaw (mandible) help in racial discrimination to a minor extent only whereas 70 to 75 per cent accuracy could be achieved through the detailed study of pelvis with regard to American Whites and Blacks (Negroes).

Long bones and scapula, on the other hand, do not help in providing any relevant racial distinction.

Following general traits have been used to distinguish the three great races of the world, viz. Caucasian, Negroes and Mongoloids, from one another (El-Najjar and McWilliams, 1978).

1. *CAUCASIAN* : The Caucasian face comes to a sharp vertical line in the median plane producing a narrow face with a hatchet like profile (hatchet face). The cheek bones (malars) recede, and the skull tends to be long with well marked depression at the nasal root. The upper ends of the nasal bones seem to disappear beneath an overhanging projection at glabella. This feature is typical of North European males and less so of Mediterraneans and females. Their face is orthognathous. Muscular markings are prominent. The orbits tend to be rounded with narrow and elongated nasal aperture. The palate is generally triangular in shape. The post cranial bones are usually heavy in comparison to other racial groups, i. e. Negroes and Mongoloids.

2. *NEGRO* : A pedomorphic skull with few knobs and a rounded forehead, light muscle markings and guttered nasal sill (hollowed opening) characterise the Negro skull. The nasal margins are usually rounded in Negro skull while among Caucasians and Mongoloids it is sharp. Another important trait in skulls of Negroes is the pronounced alveolar and facial prognathirm. Their orbits tend to be square and the nasal aperture flared. The palate may be narrow and pointed or

nearly rectangular in shape. The skull of Negroes, generally tend to be long.

3. *MONGOLOID* : The Mongoloid skull is generally round rather than long like Negroes. The cheek bones are projecting which gives a flat face appearance. The shovel shaped maxillary central incisors are the diagnostic characteristic of Mongoloids as this trait occur rarely in other races. The Mongoloid face may exhibit a slight alveolar prognathism which is not as marked as in Negroes. Their orbits are roughly triangular in shape and the nasal aperture usually tends to be rounded. The palate is generally parabolic in shape.

The aforecited traits may broadly help in discriminating the skulls into these three races but individual variations might hinder this process, as it is quite difficult to estimate the race of a skeleton.

CHAPTER 8

RECONSTRUCTION OF STATURE

Reconstruction of Stature from Skeletal Remains

Determination of stature or height of an individual when living from the available skeletal material has obvious importance for identification of the recent murder victims in decomposed or mutilated or partially mutilated state. Besides reconstruction of stature, no other identification procedure employed by forensic anthropologists has undergone such a complex course of development involving numerous identifiable researchers, from more or less detached parts of the skeleton.

J.J. Sue (1755), an anatomist, published four body measurements and maximum length of many of the bones of 14 cadavers ranging in age from a six-week old foetus to an adult of 25 years. The body measurements included—stature, trunk length, upper extremity length and lower extremity length. On the basis of these, Sue provided the first clear documentation of two main facts regarding body proportions during growth, i.e. (1) the length of the trunk exceeds that of the lower extremity until about 14 years of age, whereafter both lengths are equal (because after 14 the pubic symphysis is usually the centre of the body length), and (2) that the length of the upper extremity exceeds that of the lower until about birth, whereafter the lower extremity is usually longer than the upper. The main purpose of Sue in publishing these measurements was to provide artists with the means of rendering human body in correct proportions. M.J.B. Orfila (1821) brought wider attention to Sue's measurements through medico-legal books. Unlike Sue, Orfila used metric units to measure his series of 51 cadavers and 20 skeletons. In order to determine stature from the measurements of Sue and Orfila one required to mcasure the length of one or more bones to note the corresponding cadaver stature. In the beginning of nineteenth century British anthropologists and medico-legal experts combined Sue-Orfila measurements with their own to investigate relationship of long bone lengths to stature. Paul Broca (1859) introduced the osteometric board for accurate measurement of long bones and Paul Topinard in 1888 combined his data with that of Orfila and Humphry to calculate the average long bone-stature ratios and derived length of a given long bone, while Rollet calculated the average length of a given long bone from individuals with same stature. Manouvrier added two mm to each bone length, and then subtracted two mm from the stature thus obtained.

Thomas Dwight (1894) described two methods for the purpose of stature estimation, i.e. (1) Anatomical, and (2) Mathematical. The anatomical method involves in simply putting the bones together, in reproducing the curves of the spine, in making due allowance for the soft parts, and measuring the height. This method could be used only if a complete skeleton is available. The mathematical method, on the other hand, is based on the proportion of certain bones to the height. This method could be used by forensic anthropologists even if a single long bone is available for examination.

1. Anatomical Method for Stature Reconstruction

As mentioned above, Dwight (1894) was of the opinion that anatomical method would yield more accurate estimate of stature than any of the mathematical method developed at that time. Yet he seems to have given less thought to the practical complication, time and expertise involved in using anatomical method as the results are dependent to a great extent on skeletal completeness. Dwight's method comprises nine steps for the execution of which a stout laboratory table, long enough, for laying out a supine skeleton is required, besides good amount of modelling clay to support the individual bones in proper articulation. The various steps involved in stature estimation are as follows :

1. Making due allowance at the top end of the table for the eventual addition of the skull, embed the atlas and each succeeding verterbra down to the sacrum in a bed of clay with careful attention to the articulation of the posterior facets and thereby the reconstruction of the original curves.
2. Add the pelvis, articulating the posterior sacral facets with those of L-5 in the same manner as for the other vertebrae and taking care the anterior superior spines of the ilia are on the same horizontal plane as the spines of the pubes.
3. Place the head end of one of the femora in its acetabulum making sure that the femoral head does not touch the rim of the acetabulum and that the plane of the inferior surfaces of both condyles is at a right angle to the long axis of the table.
4. Add the tibia, leaving a space of 6 mm between it and the femur.
5. Add talus, leaving a space of 3 mm between it and the tibia.
6. Add calcaneus, leaving a space of 3 mm between it and the talus.
7. Allow 12 mm for the soft parts of the sole of the foot.
8. Add the skull to the atlas, leaving a space of 3 mm between their condyles.
9. Allow 6 mm for the thickness of the scalp.

The sum of the allowances for cartilage and external tissues in aforecited procedure amounts to 32 mm. Topinard recommended 35 mm to be added to the skeletal length for the soft parts to attain living stature of an individual.

Fully (1956) provided an alternative method for stature estimation when the complete skeletal remains are available for examination and claims that this method provides the smallest standard deviation. Under this method determination of skeletal sex is not essential to reconstruct stature, while in case of the formulae provided by Trotter and Gleser or Genoves, the sex and race determination is necessary before using the formulae of reconstruction of stature.

Fully's formula may be employed if the skeleton is complete or a few vertebrae are missing. The following table is used to obtain the average percentage contribution of each vertebra to the total height of the column (Table 10).

TABLE 10

Percentage Contribution of Each Vertebra to the Total Height of the Column

Cervical	Thoracic		Lumber
C-2=7.80	T-1=3.41	T-7=4.19	L-1=5.53
C-3=2.80	T-2=3.61	T-8=4.24	L-2=5.62
C-4=2.73	T-3=3.72	T 9=4.35	L-3=5.66
C-5=2.66	T-4=3.83	T-10=4.61	L-4=5.63
C-6=2.67	T-5=3.98	T-11=4.96	L-5=5.76
C-7=2.95	T-6=4.10	T-12=5.23	

Using the values given in Table-10 for the missing vertebra (e) and measuring the remaining, the total height of the vertebral column is derived by a simple proportionality equation. In case of combined height of the missing vertebrae exceeds beyond 20 per cent of the total column this method should not be used. Besides this, Fully used following cranial and post cranial measures for the purpose of statue reconstruction.

1. Basion-bregma height.
2. Total vertebral height (obtained as the sum of the heights of the bodies).
3. First sacral segment height (anterior carpal height of the first sacral segment).

4. Oblique length of femur.
5. Tibial length.
6. Tarsal height (articulate the talus and calcaneus and measure the distance between the superior surface of the talus and the inferior surface of the calcaneus, using osteometric board).

After obtaining these measurements they are summed together to obtain the total skeletal height. This height is used in the following regression equation to obtain antemortem stature.

Stature=0.98 (Total skeletal height)+14.63±2.05 cm.

2. Mathematical Method for Reconstruction of Stature

There have been numerous attempts by researchers to formulate means of stature reconstruction. Of passing historic note is Beddoe's (1887-88) attempt to estimate stature of the "Older Races of England" using the following formula for males.

$$X=4\left[F-\frac{1}{8}(F-13)-\frac{1}{8}(F-13-[F-19])\right]$$

$$=3F+F-\tfrac{1}{2}(F-13)-\tfrac{1}{2}F-13-[F-19])$$

$$=3F-13+\tfrac{1}{2}(F-19)$$

Where X=living stature, and

F=femur length in inches.

In case of females simply substitute 12 for 13 and 17.5 for 19.

Rollet (1888) published the earliest formal tables using humerus, radius, ulna, femur, tibia and fibula of 50 male and 50 female French cadavera by measuring the long 50 bones first in the fresh state and ten months later in the dry state and observed a loss of 2 mm in overall length during this period.

Manouvrier (1892-93) re-assessed Rollet's data by excluding 26 males and 25 females over the age of 60 years and based his prediction tables on 24 males and 25 females. The basic difference between the appraoch of these two researchers was that Manouvrier determined the average stature of individuals who presented the same length for a given long bone while Rollet determined the average length of a given long bone from individuals with the same stature.

Later in 1899, Pearson, using Rollet's data, developed regression formulae, based on bones exclusively from right side. Meanwhile the Geneva Agreement proposed regarding estimation of stature with the help of long bones recommended that the maximum bone length should be measured in all cases, except for femur, which is to be measured in oblique position. The agreement further states that tibia should also be measured obliquely excluding the spine. Pearson, who was oriented more towards prehistoric and racial reconstructions than to the forensic problems, provided the following regression formulae for males and females for estimation of living stature from dead long bones.

Males

Stature or $S=81.306+1.880$ Femur

$S=70.641+2.894$ Humerus

$S=78.664+2.376$ Tibia

$S=85.925+3.271$ Radius

$S=71.272+1.159$ (Femur+Tibia)

$S=71.443+1.220$ Femur$+1.080$ Tibia

$S=66.855+1.730$ (Humerus+Radius)

$S=66.788+2.709$ Humerus$+0.195$ Radius

$S=68.397+1.030$ Femur$+1.557$ Humerus

$S=67.049+0.913$ Femur$+0.600$ Tibia$+1.225$ Humerus-0.187 Radius

Females

Stature or $S=72.844+1.945$ Femur

$S=71.475+2.754$ Humerus

$S=74.774+2.352$ Tibia

$S=81.224+3.343$ Radius

$S=69.154+1.126$ (Femur+Tibia)

$$S=69.561+1.117\ \text{Femur}+1.125\ \text{Tibia}$$

$$S=69.911+1.628\ (\text{Humerus}+\text{Radius})$$

$$S=70.542+2.582\ \text{Humerus}+0.281\ \text{Radius}$$

$$S=67.435+1.339\ \text{Femur}+1.027\ \text{Humerus}$$

$$S=67.496+0.782\ \text{Femur}+1.120\ \text{Tibia}+1.059\ \text{Humerus}-0.711\ \text{Radius}$$

As a matter of fact Dwight did not foresee the probable improvements that were implemented by Pearson in the mathematical method for estimation of stature from the long bones. Later in 1894 Dwight attempted to reconstruct stature from vertebrae by obtaining straight line length of the whole spine (atlas to sacral promonary) and by relating this to body length derived coefficients for both the sexes. These coefficients had great utility for determining the stature of burned remains in which only the spinal column has survived intact.

Macdonnel, (1901) reported on estimation of stature from other measures than long bone lengths. He incorporated finger III length, cubit length (from elbow-to-tip of the middle finger) and foot length. The estimation formulae formulated by Macdonnel follow as under :

$$\text{Stature} = 166.45716+7.7849\ (\text{Finger III}-11.54737)$$

$$= 166.45716+2.6301\ (\text{Cubit}-45.05864)$$

$$= 166.45716+4.0301\ (\text{Foot}-25.68770)$$

$$= 166.45716-0.6703\ (\text{Finger III}-11.54737)+2.7886\ (\text{Cubit}-45.05864)$$

$$= 166.45716+2.8360\ (\text{Finger III}-1154737+3.0304\ (\text{Foot}-25.68770)$$

Pan (1924) measured 142 East Indian (Hindu) cadavera for stature and maximum lengths of humerus, radius, ulna, femur, tibia and fibula in wet state with cartilage and presented his data in terms of the length of a given bone in proportion to stature.

Paul Stevenson (1929) published regression equations for prediction of stature on the basis of data on 48 male Chinese skeletons.

Cadaver length or $C=61.7207+2.4378\ \text{Fem.}\pm2.1756$

$$C=81.5115+2.8131\ \text{Hum.}\pm2.8903$$
$$C=59.2256+3.0263\ \text{Tib.}\pm1.8916$$
$$C=80.0276+3.7384\ \text{Rad.}\pm2.6791$$
$$C=54.2522+1.4294\ (\text{Fem.}+\text{Tib.})\pm1.9214$$
$$C=63.4865+1.9222\ (\text{Hum.}+\text{Rad.})\pm2.6529$$
$$C=55.3865+0.6024\ \text{Fem.}+2.4014\ \text{Tib.}\pm1.8605$$
$$C=64.4272+1.3052\ \text{Hum.}+2.6889\ \text{Rad.}\pm2.5691$$
$$C=59.7828+2.3397\ \text{Fem.}+0.2012\ \text{Hum.}\pm2.1747$$
$$C=57.1954+2.8594\ \text{Tib.}+0.3398\ \text{Rad.}\pm1.8838$$
$$C=52.2596+0.6640\ \text{Fem.}+2.2065\ \text{Tib.}-0.1008\ \text{Hum.}+0.4464\ \text{Rad.}\pm1.8201$$

Surprisingly stevenson's equations did not work successfully with European data and neither did Pearson's equations work successfully with Chinese data.

Nat (1931) on the other hand obtained data on East Indians (United Provinces) and formulated "Multiplication Factor" for each long bone.

Bone	*Multiplication Factor (M.F.)*
Humerus	5.3
Radius	6.9
Ulna	6.3
Femur	3.7
Tibia	4.48
Fibula	4.48

further observed that these M.F.'s are applicable to the people of United Provinces only and reports that the stature could be estimated within an accuracy of ± 1 inch.

Mendes-Correa (1932) conducted a study on Portuguese

cadaver using maximum lengths of humerus, radius, ulna, femur, tibia and fibula to relate his calculations to both cadaver and a living population sample. The later was found to be consistently 20 mm shorter than the former.

Breitinger (1937) constructed following formulae for Germans, based on maximum lengths of humerus (H), radius (R), femur (F) and tibia (T) bones of 2400 male skeletons.

$$\begin{aligned} \text{Stature} &= 83.21 + 2.715\ (H) \pm 4.9\ \text{cm} \\ &= 97.09 + 2.968\ (R) \pm 5.4\ \text{cm} \\ &= 94.31 + 1.645\ (F) \pm 4.8\ \text{cm} \\ &= 94.59 + 1.988\ (T) \pm 4.7\ \text{cm} \end{aligned}$$

His formulae invariably gave higher estimates of stature as compared to the ones propounded by Manouvrier and Pearson.

Smith (1939) used diaphyseal length of fotal long bones to derive fotal stature.

$$\begin{aligned} \text{Fotal length} &= 11.30 \times \text{clavicle} \\ &= 7.60 \times \text{humerus} \\ &= 9.20 \times \text{radius} \\ &= 6.71 \times \text{femur} \\ &= 7.63 \times \text{tibia} \end{aligned}$$

Telkka (1950) studied 115 male and 39 female Finns skeleton to formulate means of stature reconstruction for both the sexes. Telkka emphasised that if bones are measured in 'wet' or 'fresh' state, two mm must be deducted from the length of each bone, as cadaver length is 2 cm greater than the standing (living) stature. Following are the formulae constructed by Telkka for the two sexes :

Males

$$\begin{aligned} \text{Stature} &= 169.4 + 2.8\ (\text{Hum.} - 32.9) \pm 5.0\ \text{cm} \\ &= 169.4 + 3.4\ (\text{Rad.} - 22.7) \pm 5.0\ \text{cm} \\ &= 169.4 + 3.2\ (\text{Uln.} - 23.1) \pm 5.2\ \text{cm} \\ &= 169.4 + 2.1\ (\text{Fem.} - 45.5) \pm 4.9\ \text{cm} \end{aligned}$$

$=169.4+2.1$ (Tib.-36.2)±4.6 cm
$=169.4+2.5$ (Fib.-36.1)±4.4 cm

Females

Stature $=156.8+2.7$ (Hum.-30.7)±3.9 cm
$=156.8+3.1$ (Rad.-20.8)±4.5 cm
$=156.8+3.3$ (Uln.-21.3)±4.4 cm
$=156.8+1.8$ (Fem.-41.8)±4.0 cm
$=156.8+1.9$ (Tib.-33.1)±4.6 cm
$=156.8+2.3$ (Fib.-32.7)±4.5 cm

Dupertuis and Hadden (1951) measured maximum lengths of humerus, radius, femur and tibia of 100 skeletons for each sex for Whites and Negroes. Their study was designed primarily as a test of the validity of the Pearsonian formulae. In their final evaluation they recommended following general formula, non-racial for males and females :

Male

Stature or $S=69.089+2.238\ F$
$S=81.688+2.392\ T$
$S=73.570+2.670\ H$
$S=80.045+3.650\ R$
$S=69.549+1.225\ (F+T)$
$S=71.294+1.728\ (H+R)$
$S=66.424+1.422\ F+1.062\ T$
$S=66.400+1.789\ H+1.841\ R$
$S=64.505+1.928\ F+0.568\ H$
$7=78.272+2.102\ T+0.606\ R$
$S=56.006+1.442\ F+0.931\ T+0.083\ H+0.480\ R$

Female

Stature or $S=61.412+2.317\ F$
$S=72.572+2.533\ T$

$$S=64.977+3{\cdot}144\ H$$
$$S=73.502+3.876\ R$$
$$S=65.213+1.233\ (F+T)$$
$$S=55.729+1.984\ (H+R)$$
$$S=59.259+1.657F+0.879\ T$$
$$S=60.344+2.164+1.525\ R$$
$$S=57.600+2.009\ F+0.566\ H$$
$$S=65.354+2.082\ T+1.060\ R$$
$$S=57.495+1.544\ F+0.764T+0.126\ H+0.295\ R$$

Although Dupertuis and Hadden (1951) were the first to publish their results, but the usage of their prediction equations was immediately superseded by that of Trotter and Gleser (1952) equations, because they had supplimented their cadaver data with the extensive data on young American dead of World War II for which stature measured in life were available. They had extended their racial coverage to the Mongoloid war deads and introduced with their equations a correction for age (Trotter and Gleser, 1951) using the under mentioned formula :

0.06 (mean age for sample—30)—(Assumed age of individual—30).

Trotter and Gleser (1952) provided following prediction equations for different racial groups.

White males

$$S=2.38\ Fem+61.41\pm3.27$$
$$S=2.52\ Tib+78.62\pm3.37$$
$$S=2.68\ Fib+71.78\pm3.29$$
$$S=3.08\ Hum.+70.45\pm4.05$$
$$S=3.78\ Rad+79.01\pm4.32$$
$$S=3.70\ Uln+74.05\pm4.32$$
$$S=1.70\ (Fem+Tib)+63.29\pm2.99$$

White females

$$S=2.47\ Fem+54.10\pm3.72$$

S=2.90 Tib+61.53±3.66
S=2.93 Fib+59.61±3.57
S=3.36 Hum+57.97±4.45
S=4.74 Rad+54.93±4.24
S=4.27 Uln+57.67±4.40
S=1.39 (Fem+Fib)+53.20±3.58

Black males

S=2.11 Fem+70.35±3.94
S=2.19 Tib+80.02±3.78
S=2.19 Fib+85.65±4.08
S=3.26 Hum+62.10±4.43
S=3.42 Rad+81.56±4.30
S=3.26 Uln+79.29+4.22
S=1.15 (Fem+Tib)+71.04±3.53

Black females

S=2.28 Fem+59,76±3.41
S=2.45 Tib+72.65±3.70
S=2.49 Fib+70.90±3.80
S=3.08 Hum+64.67±4.25
S=3.67 Rad+71.79±4.59
S=3.31 Uln+75.38±4.83
S=1.26 (Fem+Tib)+59.72±3.28

Mongoloid males

S=2.15 Fem+72.57±3.80
S=2.39 Tib+81.45±3.27
S=2.40 Fib+80.56±3.24
S=2.68 Hum+83.19±4.25
S=3.54 Rad+82.00±4.60
S=3.48 Uln+77.45±4.66
S=1.22 (Fem+Tib)+70.37±3.24

Mexican males

$$S=2.44\ \text{Fem}+58.67\pm2.99$$
$$S=2.36\ \text{Tib}+80.62\pm3.76$$
$$S=2.50\ \text{Fib}+75.44\pm3.52$$
$$S=2.92\ \text{Hum}+73.94\pm4.29$$
$$S=3.55\ \text{Rad}+80.71\pm4.04$$
$$S=3.56\ \text{Uln}+74.56\pm4.05$$

Trotter (1970) further comments that there is abundant evidence to indicate that the most accurate estimates of stature are obtained when equation applied to the unknown has been derived from a representative sample of the population of the same sex, race, age, geographical area and time period to which the unknown is believed to belong,

Estimation of stature in case of sub-adult skeletal remains is a critical problem in forensic anthropology and is less commonly attempted when dealing with archaeological specimens. Oliver (1969) constructed a prediction table for estimating sub-adult stature from length of the femoral diaphysis. Yet another study by Oliver and Pineau (1958) cited by Oliver (1969) provide regression equations for estimating foetal stature from bone length.

$$\begin{aligned}\text{Foetal stature (cm)} &= 7.92\ \text{Hum}-0.32\pm1.80\\ &= 13.80\ \text{Rad}-2.85\pm1.80\\ &= 8.73\ \text{Uln}-1.07\pm1.59\\ &= 6.29\ \text{Fem}+4.42\pm1.82\\ &= 7.85\ \text{Fib}+2.78\pm1.65\\ &= 7.39\ \text{Tib}+3,55\pm1.92\end{aligned}$$

Later Allbrook (1961) provided regression equations for estimating stature for living populations of British and East African males using percutaneous lengths of tibia and ulna. He considered four East African populations, viz. Nilohamite students, Nilohamite tribals, Nilote students and Bantu students, and British soldiers in his study and formulated the following regression equations for the prediction of stature :

1. **Nilohamite students**

$$\text{Stature} = 2.15 \text{ Tibia} + 77.74 \pm 3.76$$
$$= 1.19 \text{ Ulna} + 132.81 \pm 5.39$$

2. **Nilohamite tribals**

$$\text{Stature} = 2.00 \text{ Tibia} + 91.19 \pm 1.89$$
$$= 3.26 \text{ Ulna} + 77.94 \pm 2.97$$

3. **Nilote students**

$$\text{Stature} = 1.96 \text{ Tibia} + 89.26 \pm 3.65$$
$$= 3.59 \text{ Ulna} + 63.17 \pm 5.06$$

4. **Bantu students**

$$\text{Stature} = 2.50 \text{ Tibia} + 65.00 \pm 3.73$$
$$= 3.24 \text{ Ulna} + 72.31 \pm 4.65$$

5. **British soldiers**

$$\text{Stature} = 2.30 \text{ Tibia} + 83.78 \pm 3.46$$
$$= 3.06 \text{ Ulna} + 88.94 \pm 4.38$$

On Western Europeans, Lorke et al. (1953) and on Japanese, Fujii (1958) provided respective prediction equations for stature estimation. Genoves (1966 ; 1967) used 69 male and 29 female American Indian dissecting room cadavers and formulated regression formulae for estimating stature among Mongoloids.

In India, Athwale (1963) constructed regression equations for adult Maharashtrian males (living) using radiological technique for measuring the length of living bones on the skiagram.

Patel et. al. (1964), and Joshi et al. (1964 ; 1965) formulated the following regression equations for prediction of stature healthy adult males of Medical College, Baroda (Gujarat) using percutaneous lengths of tibia and Ulna :

$$\text{Stature} = 65.51 + 2.203 \text{ Tibia} \pm .74 \text{ Age}$$
$$= 55.42 + 3.506 \text{ Ulna} \pm .027 \text{ Age}$$

=80.97+2.206 Tibia±8.15
=70.88+3.506 Ulna±9.98
=51.61+1.79 Tibia+1.66 Ulna±7.64

Badkur (1985) on the basis of the maximum length of six long bones belonging to 82 male and62 female Indian skeletons, from Madhya Pradesh, formulated the following regression equations :

Males

Stature=1209.15+1.44 Humerus±27.4 mm
=1305.15+1.45 Radius±30.4 mm
=1294.55+1.39 Ulna±30.9 mm
=994.11+1.52 Femur±16.3 mm
=987.62+1.78 Tibia±19.0 mm
=976.92+1.88 Fibula±20.9 mm

Females

Stature=1010.48+1.77 Humerus±25.6 mm
=1023.34+2.22 Radius±27.4 mm
=1003.06+2.14 Ulna±28.3 mm
=900.42+1.53 Femur±16.7 mm
=923.06+1.75 Tibia±21.6 mm
=926.29+1.79 Fibula±21.6 mm.

Besides these, she also formulated multiple regression equations incorporating all the bones in different combinations for increasing accuracy in prediction of stature on Indian skeletal material.

Multiple regression equations for estimating stature (in mm) from different long bone lengths for males are :

Male	R	r
S=832.58−0.01 (Hum)—0,03 (Rad) —0.04 (Ulna)+1.01 (Fem) —0.99 (Tib)+0.08 (Fib) ±8.39	0.974	
S=832.78—0.01 (Hum)—0.06 (Rad) —0.02 (Ulna)+1.04 (Fem) +1.03 (Tib)±8.47	0.973	

	R	r
S=828.95—0.01 (Hum)—0.08 (Rad) +1.02 (Fem)+1.00 (Tib) +0.09 (Fib)±8.44	0.974	
S=835.11—0.02 (Hum)—0.04 (Rad) +1.03 (Fem)+1.03 (Tib) ±8.37	0.973	
S=891.22+0.17 (Hum)−0.23 (Rad) +1.07 (Fem)+0.83 (Fib) ±13.48	0.930	
S=1146.92+0.92 (Hum+Rad)±27.29		0.658
S=1161.47+0.86 (Hum+Ulna)±27.43		0.653
S=1274.08+0.75 (Rad+Ulna)±30.97		0.523
S=820.25+1.01 (Fem)+1.02 (Tib) ±8.33	0.973	
S=883.82+1.08 (Fem)+0.83 (Fib) ±13.62	0.927	
S=830.52+1.02 (Fem+Tib)±8.31		0.973
S=875.17+0.98 (Fem+Fib)±13.69		0.926
S=897.24+0.99 (Tib+Fib)±16.85		0.887

Multiple regression equations for estimating stature (in mm) from different long bones for females are :

Female	R	r
S=774.90—0.03 (Hum)+0.34 (Rad) —0.27 (Ulna)+0.99 (Fem) +0.50 (Tib)+0.50 (Fib) ±9.26	0.975	
S=775.48—0.02 (Hum)+0.34 (Rad) −0.14 (Ulna)+1.00 (Fem) +0.82 (Tib)±9.98	0.970	
S=768.77—0.04 (Hum)+0.11 (Rad) +1.00 (Fem)+0.51 (Tib) +0.47 (Fib)±9.31	0.974	
S=772.20—0.12 (Hum)+0.21 (Rad) +1.01 (Fem)+0.86 (Tib) ±9.96	0.970	
S=784.64+0.05 (Hum)—0.03 (Ulna) +1.04 (Fem)+0.92 (Fib) ±10.17	0.969	

TABLE-11

Comparative listing of regression equations for estimation of stature from different bone lengths for the two sexes.

Bone	Auther/Race	Male	Female
Humerus	Badkur (1985) M.P. Indians	S=1209.15+1.44 (Hum)±27.4	S=1010.48+1.77 (Hum)±25.6
	Pearson (1899) French	S=706.40+2.89 (Hum)	S=714.80+2.75 (Hum)
	Stevenson (1929) Chinese	S=825.10+2.81 (Hum)±21.80	—
	Breitinger (1937) Germans	S=832.10+2.72 (Hum)±49.0	—
	Telkka (1950) Finns	S=752.80+2.80 (Hum)±50.0	S=719.10+2.70 (Hum)±39.0
	Dupertuis & Hadden (1951) Whites	S=983.40+2.27 (Hum)	S=567.30+3.45 (Hum)
	Dupertuis & Hadden (1951) Negroes	S=502.60+3.71 (Hum)	S=699.80+3.03 (Hum)
	Trotter and Gleser (1952) Whites	S=704.50+3.08 (Hum)±40.5	S=579.70+3.36 (Hum)±44.5
	Trotter aad Gleser (1952) Negroes	S=621.00+3.26 (Hum)±44.3	S=646.70+3.08 (Hum)±42.5
	Trotter and Gleser (1958) Whites	S=781.00+3.89 (Hum)±45.7	—
	Trotter and Gleser (1958) Negroes	S=754.80+2.88 (Hum)±42.3	—
	Trotter and Gleser (1958) Mongoloids	S=831.90+2.68 (Hum)±42.5	—
	Trotter and Gleser (1958) Mexicans	S=739.40+2.92 (Hum)±42.4	—

Radius	Badkur (1985)	M.P. Indians	S=1305.15+1.45 (Rad)±30.42	S=1023.34+2.22 (Rad)±27.4
	Pearson (1899)	French	S=859.30+3.27 (Rad)	S=812.20+3.34 (Rad)
	Stevenson (1929)	Chinese	S=820.30+3 74 (Rad)	—
	Breitinger (1937)	Germans	S=970.90+2.97 (Rad)±54.0	—
	Telkka (1950)	Finns	S=902.20+3.40 (Rad)±50.0	S=903.20+3.10 (Rad)±45.0
	Dupertuis and Hadden (1951)	Whites	S=888.80+3.50 (Rad)	S=682.40+4.26 (Rad)
	Dupertutis and Hadden (1951)	Negrocs	S=691.70+4.04 (Rad)	S=749.10+3.76 (Ra)
	Trotter and Gleser (1952)	Whites	S=790.10+3.78 (Rad)	S=549.30+4.74 (Rad)
	Trotter and Gleser (1952)	Negroes	S=851.60+3.42 (Rad)±43.0	S=945.10+2 75 (Rad)
	Trotter and Gleser (1958)	Whites	S=794.20+3.79 (Rad)±46.6	—
	Trotter and Gleser (1958)	Negroes	S=854.30+3.32 (Rad)±45.7	—
	Trotter and Gleser (1958)	Mongoloids	S=820.00+3.54 (Rad)±46.0	--
	Trotter and Gleser (1958)	Mexicans	S=807.10+3.55 (Rad)±40.4	—
Ulna	Badkur (1985)	M.P. Indians	S=1294.55+1.39 (Ulna)±30.98	S=1003.06+2.14 (Ulna)±28.3
	Pearson (1899)	French	—	—
	Stevenson (1929)	Chinese	—	—
	Breitinger (1937)	Germans	—	—
	Telkka (1950)	Finnis	S=934.00+3.20 (Ulna)±52.0	S=845.10 +3.30 (Ulna)±44.0

	Dupertuis and Hadden (1951) Whites		—	—
	Dupertuis and Hadden (1951) Negroes		—	—
	Trotter and Gleser (1952) Whites		S=740.50+3.70 (Ulna)±43.20	S=577.60+4.27 (Ulna)±43.0
	Trotter and Gleser (1952) Negroes		S=792.90+3.26 (Ulna)±44.2	S=753.80+3.31 (Ulna)±48.3
	Trotter and Gleser (1958) Whites		S=755.50+2.76 (Ulna)±47.2	—
	Trotter and Gleser (1958) Negroes		S=827.70+3.20 (Ulna)±47.4	—
	Trotter and Gleser (1958) Mongoloids		S=774.50+3.48 (Ulna)±46.6	—
	Trotter and Gleser (1958) Mnxicans		S=745.60+3.56 (Ulna)±40.5	—
Femur	Badkur (1985)	M.P. Indians	S=994.11+1.52 (Fem)±16.30	S=900.42+1.53 (Fem)±16.71
	Pearson (1899)	French	S=813.10+1 88 (Fem)	S=728.40+1.95 (Fem)
	Stevenson (1929)	Chinese	S=637.20+2.44 (Fem)±21.8	—
	Breitinger (1937)	Germans	S=9.43.10+1.64 (Fem)±48.0	—
	Telkka (1950)	Finns	S=718.50+2.10 (Fem)±49.0	S=791.60+1.80 (Fem)±40.0
	Dupertuis and Hadden (1951) Whites		S=770.50+2.12 (Fem)	S=628.70+2.32 (Fem)
	Dupertuis and Hadden (1951) Negroes		S=550.20+2.54 (Fem)	S=542.40+2.50 (Few)
	Trotter and Gleser (1952) Whites		S=614.10+2.38 (Fem)±32.7	S=540.00+2.47 (Fem)±37.2
	Trotter and Gleser (1952) Negroes		S=703.50+2.11 (Fem)±39.4	S=597.60+2.28 (Fem)±34.1
	Trotter and Gleser (1958) Whites		S=655.30+2.32 (Fem)±39.4	—
	Trotter and Gleser (1958) Negroes		S=722.20+2.10 (Fem)±39.1	—

	Trotter and Gleser (1958)	Mongoloids	S=725.70+2.15 (Fem)±38.0	—
	Trotter and Gleser (1958)	Mexicans	S=586.70+2.44 (Fem)±29.9	—
Tibia	Badkur (1985)	M.P. Indians	S=987.62+1.78 (Tib)±19.00	S=923.06+1.75 (Tib)±27.6
	Pearson (1899)	French	S=786.60+2.38 (Tib)	S=747.79+2.35 (Tib)
	Stevenson (1929)	Chinese	S=612.20+3.03 (Tib)	—
	Breitinger (1937)	Germans	S=955.90+1.99 (Tib)±47.0	—
	Telkka (1950)	Finns	S=913.80+2.10 (Tib)±46.0	S=919.10+1.90 Tib)±46.0
	Dupertuis and Hadden (1951)	Whites	S=927.70+2.18 (Tib)	S=716.50+2.64 (Tib)
	Dupertuis and Hadden (1951)	Negroes	S=721.20+2.61 (Tib)	S=723.90+2.52 (Tib)
	Trotter and Gleser (1952)	Whites	S=786.20+2.52 (Tib)±33.7	S=615.30+2.90 (Tib)±36.6
	Trotter and Gleser (1952)	Negroes	S=860.20+2.19 (Tib)±37.8	S=726.50+2.45 (Tib)±37.0
	Trotter and Gleser (1958)	Whites	S=819.30+2.42 (Tri)±40.0	—
	Trotter and Gleser (1958)	Negroes	S=853.60+2.19 (Tib)±39.6	—
	Trotter and Gleser (1958)	Mongoloids	S=814.50+2.39 (Tib)±32.7	—
	Trotter and Gleser (1958)	Mexicans	S=806.20+2.36 (Tib)±37.3	—
Fibula	Badkur (1985)	M.P. Indians	S=976.92+1.88 (Fib)±20.9	S=926.29+1.79 (Fib)±21.6
	Pearson (1899)	French	—	—

Author	Population		
Stevenson (1929)	Chinese	—	—
Breitinger (1937)	Germans	—	—
Telkka (1950)	Finns	S=764.50+2.50 (Fib)±44.0	S=918.70+2.30 (Fib)±45.0
Dupertuis and Hadden (1951)	Whites	—	—
Dupertuis and Hadden (1951)	Negroes	—	—
Trotter and Gleser (1952)	Whites	S=717.80+2.68 (Fib)±32.9	S=596.10+2.93 (Fib)±35.7
Trotter and Gleser (1952)	Negroes	S=856.50+2.19 (Fib)±40.8	S=709.0+2.49 (Fib)±38.0
Trotter and Gleser (1958)	Whites	S=755.00+2.60 (Fib)±38.6	—
Trotter and Gleser (1958)	Negroes	S=800.70+2.34 (Fib)±40.2	—
Trotter and Gleser (1958)	Mongoloids	S=805.60+2.40 (Fib)±34.2	—
Trotter and Gleser (1958)	Mexicans	S=754.40+2.50 (Fib)±35.2	—

$S=941.82+1.12\ (Hum+Rad)\pm23.71$		0.811
$S=923.06+1.12\ (Hum+Ulna)\pm24.00$		0.806
$S=995.95+1.13\ (Rad+Ulna)\pm27.34$		0.739
$S=780.99+1.06\ (Fem)+0.90\ (Tib)\pm10.06$	0.969	
$S=784.30+1.05\ (Fem)+0\text{-}92\ (Fib)\pm10.10$	0.969	
$S=778.52+0.99\ (Fem+Tib)\pm10.12$		0.968
$S=782.39+1.00\ (Fem+Fib)\pm10.12$		9.968
$S=894.25+0.93\ (Tib+Fib)\pm20.28$		0.866

Table 11 presents a comparative account of different regression equations formulated by different researchers on various skeletal populations of the world. These equations exhibit great variability and further strengthen the view that they should not be used interchangeably for estimating stature. The regression equations are of particularistic importance, i.e. their predictability is context bound, and a set of regression equations is untenable in another population.

Skeletal remains from Indian subcontinent were studied for stature reconstruction by Pan (1924), Nat (1931), Siddiqui and Shah (1944), Singh and Sohal (1952) and Badkur (1985). All these researchers formulated multiplication factors (M.F.) for the prediction of stature from length of long bones (Table-12).

TABLE 12

Multiplication Factors for Prediction of Stature Among Various Indian Population Groups

Population group	Authors	Multiplication Factors					
		Hum.	Rad.	Uln.	Fem.	Tib.	Fib.
Bengalees	Pan, 1924	5.3	6.7	6.0	3.8	4.4	4.4
Upites	Nat, 1931	5.3	6.9	6.3	3.7	4.48	4.48
Punjabis (Lahore)	Siddiqui & Shah, 1944	5.0	6.5	6.0	3.6	4.2	4.4
Punjabis (Amritsar)	Singh & Sohal, 1952	4.97	6.43	5.93	3.57	4.18	4.35
M. P. Indians (Bhopal)	Badkur, 1985	5.31	6.78	6.29	3.78	4.41	4.56

Kolte and Bansal (1974) formulated regression formulae predicting stature from long bones of upper extremity, i.e. humerus, radius and ulna on a sample drawn from Mysore and Maharashtrians while Kate and Majumdar (1976) used femur for this purpose.

Duggal and Nath (1986) and Nath et al. (1987) reported on the reconstruction of stature among two tribal group of West Bengal, viz. Lodhas and Mundas. They used percutaneous length of radius, ulna and tibia and measured both sexes of the two groups to construct multiplication factors (M.F.) for the prediction of stature. The multiplication factors derived by them are as under (Table-13).

TABLE 13

Multiplication Factors based on Percutaneous Lengths of Three Bones for Lodha and Munda Tribal Groups

Population	Multiplication Factors		
	Radius	Ulna	Tibia
Lodha, males	6.40	6.01	4.23
Lodha, females	6.63	6.18	4.27
Munda, males	6.35	5.97	4.17
Munda, females	6.50	6.08	4.19

Nath and Satish Chandra (1986) also constructed the following multiplication factors using percutaneous length of radius and tibia among the Bhii males of Udaipur, Rajasthan.

Bone length	M.F.
Radius	= 6.32
Tibia	= 4.27

They have further stated that in an absence of the skeletal material of different population groups in India, it is not possible to reconstruet stature using any regression formulae or multiplication factors. In order to have some record of different population groups of India, therefore, percutaneous bone lengths are of immense use as they help in constructing regression formulae and multiplication factors for stature reconstruction.

Using percutaneous lengths of radius, ulna and tibia, Nath (1988) formulated the following regression equations for prediction of stature for Lodha males ((N=119) of district Midnapore, West Bengal :

$$\text{Stature} = 77.509 + 3.261\ \text{Radius} \pm 3.76$$
$$= 74.542 + 3.179\ \text{Ulna} \pm 3.94$$
$$= 63.961 + 2.517\ \text{Tibia} \pm 4.08$$

Considering the percutaneous lengths of thigh, tibia and upper arm (UAL) Nath (1988) formulated multiple regression equations for two tribal groups of Madhya Pradesh, viz. the Baigas and the Gonds.

The Baigas

$$\text{Stature} = 19.95 + 5.50\ \text{UAL} \pm 9.46$$
$$= 17.13 + 3.08\ \text{UAL} + 1.62\ \text{Tibia} \pm 7.66$$
$$= 17.10 + 2.71\ \text{UAL} + 0.42\ \text{Thigh} + 1.38\ \text{Tibia} \pm 7.54$$

2. **The Gonds**

$$\text{Stature} = 36.46 + 3.13\ \text{UAL} \pm 4.55$$
$$= 31.93 + 2.01\ \text{Tibia} + 1.05\ \text{Thigh} \pm 3.99$$
$$= 18.27 + 1.45\ \text{Tibia} + 0.87\ \text{Thigh} + 1.78\ \text{UAL} \pm 7.54$$

Trotter and Gleser (1958) suggested that following precautions need to be observed for reconstructing stature from bone lengths.

1. Do not combine formulae obtained by different investigators, based on different races or populations in different geographical areas, nor pertinent to different generations.
2. Do not estimate stature by determining the average of estimates obtained from several equations, each of which is based on a different bone or on a combination of bones.
3. Do not plot estimated stature against observed stature in order to test the precision of regression equations.

It is further suggested that the regression formulae or multiplication factors of one or another type have a restricted scope as they are primarily derived for a particular population. Inter-population comparisons and computation of stature from these is not possible. Every formula has a specific utility ; it is applicable for a population rather than inter-population studies.

In the calculation of stature it is advised to use more than one long bone. The leg bones (femur and tibia), if available, should be preferred over arm bones (humerus and radius) for stature estimation. Leg bones as compared to the arm bones provide better estimates.

3. Reconstruction of Stature from Bone Fragments

Muller (1935) provided a method for reconstruction of bone length from fragmentary measures of humerus, radius and tibia. He divided these three bones in the following sections :

Humerus

1. the most proximal point of humerus ;
2. the most inferior margin of the articular surface of the head ;
3. the convergence of the muscle lines originating from the greater and lesser tubercles ;
4. a transverse line passing through the proximal edge of of the olecranon fossa ;
5. a transverse line passing through the distal edge of the olecranon fossa ;
6. the most distal point of humerus.

Radius

1. the most proximal point of the radius ;
2. the inferior margin of the radial head ;
3. a transverse line passing through the middle of the radial tuberosity ;
4. the distal epiphyseal line ; and
5. the most distal point of the radius.

Tibia

1. the most proximal point of tibia ;

2. the proximal epiphyseal line ;
3. a transverse line passing through the elevated point of tuberosity ;
4. a transverse line passing through the proximal end of the anterior crest of the shaft ;
5. a transverse line passing through the point of smallest circumference of the shaft ;
6. the inferior epiphyseal line ;
7. the inferior articular surface of the tibia ; and
8. the most distal point of the medial malleolus.

It is suggested that one should measure the length of the available section of any of these three bones and using a table assess as to what percentage does the measured section contribute to the total length of the bone. The bone length thus obtained is used to calculate stature using appropriate stature estimation formula for the Europeans.

Steele and Mckern (1969) attempted to improve Muller's (1935) method for application with greater accuracy to American Indians. They considered femur, humerus and tibia and divided them into following sections :

Femur

1. the most proximal point of the head ;
2. the mid-point of the lesser trochanter ;
3. the most proximal extension of the popliteal surface at point where medial and lateral supra-condylar lines become parallel below the linea aspara ;
4. the most proximal point of the intercondylar fossa ; and
5. the most distal point of the medial condyle.

Humerus

1. the most proximal point of the head ;
2. the most distal point of the circumference of the head ;
3. the most narrowest diameter anteriorly/posteriorly when measured proximally to the deltoid tuberosity and distally to the greater tuberosity crest ;
4. the proximal margin of the olecranon fossa ;
5. the distal margin of the olecranon fossa ; and
6. the most distal point of the trochlea.

Tibia

1. the most proximal point of the inter-condylar eminence ;
2. the most proximal point of the tibial tuberosity ;
3. the point of confluence of the lines extending from the lower end of the tuberosity ;
4. the point at which the anterior crest of the tibia crosses over to the medial border of the shaft above the medial malleolus (the measurement is taken properly at the point where the crest crosses the mid-section of the shaft) ;
5. the proximal margin of the inferior articular facet (measured at the point opposite the medial malleolus) ; and
6. the most distal point of the medial malleolus.

After measuring the segment length of the bone, the following table (Table-14) is referred to obtain the per cent contribution of the segment to the total length of the bone. Once the segment length and the percent length are known, parallel length is calculated by using the following formula :

$$\text{Parallel length} = \frac{\text{Segment length}}{\text{Percent total length}} \times 100$$

The parallel length thus obtained is converted to the maximum length using the following conversion factors.

TABLE 14

Percent total lengths of segments and combination of segments of Femur, Humerus and Tibia bones (Based on data on American Indian (Steele and McKern, 1969).

Segment/ segment combin- ation	Mean Per cent total length (Males	Mean S.D. (Males)	Mean Per cent total length (Females)	Mean S.D. (Females)	Combined Percentage
			FEMUR		
1	16.4	1.1	15.6	1.1	16.1
2	56.1	2.5	56.7	2.6	56.3
3	19.4	2.5	19.6	2.4	19.5

4	7.9	0.7	7.9	.7	7.9
1—2	72.5	2.6	72.3	2.2	72.4
2—3	75.5	1.3	76.3	1.2	75.8
3—4	27.3	2.6	27.5	2.2	27.4
1—3	91.9	0.7	91.9	0.7	91.9
2—4	83.5	1.1	84.1	1.1	83.6
		HUMERUS			
1	10.5	0.8	10.1	1.0	10.3
2	22.6	2.2	22.0	1.7	22.4
3	54.6	2.4	55.1	3.0	54.7
4	8.1	0.7	8.3	0.8	8.1
5	4.3	0.5	4.5	1.0	4.4
1—2	33.0	2.3	32.1	2.2	32.7
2—3	77.1	1.3	77.1	2.0	77.1
3—4	62.6	2.4	63.4	2.7	62.9
4—5	12.4	0.8	12.8	1.3	12.5
1—3	7.6	0.8	87.2	1.3	87.5
2—4	85.2	1.1	85.4	1.6	85-3
3—5	67.0	2.3	67.9	2.2	67.2
1—4	95.7	0.5	95.5	0.9	95.6
2—5	89.5	0.8	89.9	1.1	89.6
		TIBIA			
1	6.8	1.1	6.5	1.1	6.7
2	17.5	2.9	16.5	2.9	17.2
3	47.9	3.5	49.2	4.0	48.3
4	25.1	2.2	24.7	2.6	24.9
5	4.2	0.7	4.2	0.6	4.2
1—2	24.3	2.8	23.0	2.4	23.9
2—3	65.4	2.4	65.8	2.0	65.5
3—4	73.0	2.7	73.9	2.1	73.3
4—5	29.2	2.3	28.9	2.4	29.1
1—3	72.2	2.1	72.3	2.3	72.3
2—4	90.5	1.5	90.5	1.6	90.5
3—5	77.2	2.8	78.1	2.1	77.5
1—4	97-3	0.9	97.0	0.9	97.2
2—5	94.6	1.4	94.7	1.5	94.6

Femur : Male and female maximum length = Parallel length +0.09 cm

Humerus : Male and female maximum length = Parallel length.
Tibia : Male maximum length = Parallel length—0.54 cm
: Female maximum length = Parallel length—0.04 cm.

Besides this method of bone length reconstruction from bone fragments, Steele and McKern (1969) and Steele (1970) have also formulated direct regression equations for estimating living stature from bone fragments (segments) for both the sexes of American Indian, Caucasian, and Negroes.

Badkur (1985) formulated linear regression equations for prediction of stature from various fragmentary measures of all the six long bones for both the sexes of the Indian skeletal material from Madhya Pradesh. These equations are useful in determining stature from a bone fragment depending upon their availability and the condition of the recovered bones.

1. **Humerus**

Male

Stature = 1527.89 + 2.25 Bicondylar Breadth ± 34.7 mm
= 1430.97 + 5.72 Transverse Diameter of Head ± 33.7 mm
= 1475.27 + 4.26 Vertical Diameter of Head ± 34.1 mm

Female

Stature = 1258.63 + 5.06 Bicondylar Breadth ± 33.8 mm
= 1200.25 + 9.08 Transverse Diameter of Head ± 30.6 mm
= 1203.96 + 8.28 Vertical Diameter of Head ± 31.9 mm

2. **Radius**

Male

Stature = 1484.90 + 8.45 Transverse Diameter of Head ± 33.5 mm
= 1532.31 + 5.28 Height of Radial Tuberosity ± 33.5 mm

Female

Stature = 1327.32 + 10.91 Transverse Diameter of Head ± 34.6 mm
= 1456.30 + 3.62 Height of Radial Tuberosity ± 38.8 mm

3. **Ulna**

Male

Stature =1537.34+5.10 Breadth of Olecranon ±33.9 mm
=1581.44+6.73 Height of Radial Facet ± 34.3 mm

Female

Stature =1334.97+8.98 Breadth of Olecranon ± 35.2 mm
=1432.60+9.97 Height of Radial Facet ±36.8 mm

4. **Femur**

Male

Stature =1315.26+4.18 Mid Shaft Circumference ± 27.9 mm
=1385.26+7.69 Height of Patellar Surface ± 29.7 mm
=1391.34+3.55 Bicondylar Breadth±32.0 mm

Female

Stature =1234.80+3.91 Mid Shaft Circumference ± 31.4 mm
=1261.91+8.32 Height of Patellar Surface ± 34.5 mm
=1180.03+5.05 Bicondylar Breadth ±31.1 mm

5. **Tibia**

Male

Stature =1389.91+3.80 Upper end Breadth ±32.3 mm
=1412.78+3.15 Mid-Shaft Diameter ±30.6 mm

Female

Stature =1196.68+5.17 Upper end Breadth ±32.1 mm
=1354.68+2.58 Mid-Shaft Diameter ±36.9 mm

6. Fibula

Male

Stature =1475.28+7.81 Lower Epiphyseal Breadth ± 32.7 mm

=1587.01+5.80 Mid-Shaft Circumference ± 34.9 mm

Female

Stature =1322.53+9.78 Lower Epiphyseal Breadth ± 35.3 mm

=1375.01+4.36 Mid-Shaft circumference ± 36.8 mm

CHPTER 9

ASSESSMENT OF TIME AND CAUSE OF DEATH

Besides establishing age, sex, stature, etc. of the skeletal material the forensic anthropologists in collaboration with medical professionalists require to estimate the time interval since death and the cause of death. The general impression on these aspects come primarily from observing the presence or absence of the following :

a) odour, and its intensity,
b) soft parts, and their location,
c) adherent earth (clay, loam or sand, etc.)
d) adherent vegetation (leaves, grass, twigs, etc.)
e) adherent insects, living or dead, including immature stages,
f) stains and/or bleaching, and
g) adipocere.

Under normal conditions the odour of decay persists beyond the loss of the soft parts, of which the joint cartilage is usually the last to disappear. In case a joint cartilage remains after disappearance of odour it is usually dry and hard. On the other hand, hair, which does not produce decay odour, last a long time, even in the grave, but not always collected along with the bones. The remaining observations listed above help mainly to establish where the process of skeletonisation took place and the level of temperature during the period prior to the date when the remains were recovered.

The place where skeletonisation takes place is important than any other factors because it helps in determining the number and variety of necrophagous insects that are attracted to the corpse and thus become the main agents of tissue decomposition. According to Laclercq (1969) the changes in an exposed corpse that follow rapidly on the disappearance of *rigor mortis* involve autolysis and putrifaction. It is also important to observe the richness of the local insect fauna, the upper range of the temperature, and the ecological surroundings represented by the corpse at different stages of its deterioration. Entomologists have succeeded in estimating the time since death from the infesting insects, and especially from the rates at which these insects, reproduce. However, apparently the success of this method of establishing time since death diminishes rapidly after the initial wave of infestation has been established for three weeks or so. However, the insect remains recovered with buried human remains usually reflect only the time that elapsed between death and burial, because, except before and during the process of burial, such a corpse is inaccessible to insects.

Forensic anthropologists are likely to come across, insect remains only in cases that are still incompletely skeletonised after exposure to open. Under such circumstances he or she must consult a qualified entomologist for interpretation with regard to the duration of the time since death.

1. Time of Death

Estimation of time since death, in case of skeletonised remains, is usually a guess. Although the remains that stink and the bones are partly covered with flesh represent recent death in comparison to those with less odour of decay and with no soft parts attached excepting traces of cartilage, the problem is to translate these and other stages of advanced deterioration into specific intervals of postmortem time. It has often been observed that under the most favourable circumstances a corpse will be almost completely skeletonized by the end of two weeks from the time of death. On the other hand, the skeletal remains that are shielded become skeletonised at a much slower rate, depending upon the circumstances (Stewart, 1979).

Early chemical studies of adipocere led to the belief that this material is a form of soap that depends for its formation on long emersion of a corpse in water. According to Mant and Furbank (1957) adipocere is known to consists mainly of fatty acids formed by the postmortem hydrolysis and hydrogenation of body fats. This accounts for the fact that ad'pocere is often admixed with remains of the non-fatty soft parts. The changes in adipocere begin to occur only a few days after death, but does not become visible for about three months. The presence of moisture is still regarded as a prerequisite for the change. Running water may retard the process, while a well nourished body may contain sufficient water content to permit the transformation to be carried forward. Since adipocere, once formed, is relatively permanent, its excessive formation may preserve the surface features of a body for years.

To arrive at the relative age of archaeological bone specimen the best measure is to estimate their residual nitrogen content. According to Ortner et al. (1972) the protein content of the bone, at death, begins to hydrolyse to peptides, which inturn breaks down to their constituent amino acids. The rate of degradation process depends, to a large extent, upon the prevailing temperature, water content, and pH of this water. Of all the bone constituents only protein contain nitrogen. Different researchers are of the opinion that the estimation of residual bone nitrogen would offer a measure of the length of time since death. For example, Cook and Heizer (1947) found a normal human femur from a fresh cadaver, contains 4.08 percent nitrogen, in contrast to archaeological skeletal remains from California (nearly 500 years old) had on average nitrogen content as 1.87 percent. Which further declines to 0.49 percent in about 1000 years old bones.

2. Cause of Death

A forensic anthropologist is generally questioned, after he

or she has completed examination of a skeleton, regarding the cause of death. Answer to such a question, can seldom be in affirmation with any assurance as individuals can survive massive bone damage and then die or be put to death in a different way that leaves no sign on the skeleton. Keeping this in view forensic anthropologists simply describe any evidence of bone damage, point out its placement in relation to vital centres, describe the possibility of its having been sustained at the time of death or otherwise, and discuss the likely types of objects that produced the damage.

Regarding signs of blows one can speak quite confidently of the way in which bone damage was inflected than of the effect this damage had caused upon the individual's vitality. Generally speaking, the nature of bone damage depends upon the shape of the object that struck the body and upon, the force with which the object was propelled. For example, a blow from a blunt object to the vault of the living head will produce different effects depending mainly on the location of the point and the centre of the impact. But in the dried skull evidence that a blow had been received will not be seen unless the force of the blow was great enough to cause fracture in the bone. In such a situation an understanding of the mechanism of skull fracture will help a forensic anthropologist in formulating an opinion regarding location of the point of impact. Regarding patterning of skull fractures Gurdjian et. al. (1950) describe that the area around the point of impact is inbended. Simultaneously there is an outbending of the bone perepheral to the inbended area. This outbending is selective and may be localised to a certain part of skull, where a linear fracture is initiated due to the resultant tearing-apart forces. The fracture then extends towards the point of impact and in the opposite direction. Extension is directly towards the region of impact rather than to one or the other side, because, although initially this area is in compression (bent in), it rebounds immediately after the energy of the blow has been absorbed it becomes an area of tensile stress. A fracture which has started at a considerable distance will, of course, propagate in a direction normal to the greatest tensile stress. Therefore, it must travel towards the centre of the area of impact. If insufficient energy was expended in the blow, the fracture may remain limited and not reach the point of impact. The fracture lines at a distance from the point of impact are frequently referred to as fracture by contre-coup. This reflects the existing belief that the force of the blow was transmitted from the point of impact directly through the head to the area of bone breakage, thereby simulating a counter blow.

An exception to the simple bone breaks in the matter of lethal connotation is one that involves the hyoid bone and/or the variably ossified thyroid cartilage, both located in the anterior part of neck. Interruptions to the normal continuity of these bony structures discovered after death may mean that a constricting force was applied to the neck and death was caused by strangulation. The hyoid is situated above the thyroid cartilage, which is the largest of the nine cartilages making up the so-called laryngeal skeleton. The hyoid is a concave, ovoid-shaped body from which on each side an elongated horn (greater cornu) extends postero-superiorly and in front of this a short stubby horn (lesser cornu) extends superiorly, the mature bone is U-shaped. Maturity in this instance comes in middle age when the two greater cornua unite with body. The lesser seldom fuse with body, thus its free state should not be mistaken for evidence of fracture.

The thyroid is prominent due to the thyroid laminae (Adam's Apple). Attached posteriorly to each of these laminae are two cornua, a long one superiorly and a short one inferiorly. Ossification of thyroid is said to begin around 20 years of age and to continue erratically into old age. However, the relative frequency of fracture of the two bones in forensic cases is not clearly established.

CHPTER 10

RECONSTRUCTION OF FACE

A skull, on examination, may not only tell of sex, of age, of race and thus partly contribute to cranial identification, but it may also help in revealing physical appearance of the person to whom it belongs to. This problem of skull to head reconstruction has three main aspects, i.e. comparison of the skull with portraits of the presumed deceased, comparison of the skull with photographs of the presumed deceased, and actual restoration of a head from the skull.

1. Reconstruction of the Soft Parts

There are two basic approaches to skeletal indentification through reconstruction of the soft parts of the face.

A. The reconstruction of these soft parts on the skull of an unknown as they are supposed to have looked in life either indirectly by means of a two-dimensional portrait made from the skull, or directly by means of clay applied to form a three-dimensional portrait, and

B. The comparison of the skull of an unknown with a picture of a suspect made in life by superimposition of an outline of the skull, suitably scaled and oriented, on an outline of the picture.

These methods can be considered starting directly from

opposite points. The first starts with a skull and arranges the soft parts on it in anattempt to achieve a recognizable likeness, whereas the second starts with the soft parts in the form of a purported likeness and arranges an overlay of the skull in an attempt to appraise the goodness of fit and hence the likelihood of actual association (Stewart, 1979). The literature on these methods exhibit clear evidence that both involve subjectivity to a high degree. When the effort by one means or the other has led to an identification, only little attention has been focused on whether or not the likeness *per se* had anything to do with it. Thus both the methods are surrounded by an aura of glamour that may not always be required. In general, the first method requires the skills of an artist more than those of a forensic anthropologist, while the reverse is true for the second method.

When an artist attempts to make a picture of a skull as to what that individual looked like in life, the only additional information that he or she usually has to proceed is that which the forensic anthropologist has provided regarding the age, sex and race of the unknown individual through skeletal examination. Without having any idea regarding unknown individuals clothing sizes, the degree of fleshiness is a matter of guess. Other things like face proportions, details of the features, and the amount and arrangement of hair, etc., must be developed subjectively by the artist with minimum help from the skeletal material.

Physical anthropologists have greater inclination towards the three-dimensional approach than to the two-dimensional one, because of greater control over tissue thickness that the former approach provides. In this regard, Welcker (1883). His (1895) and Kollmann (1898) are generally credited with being the first to put the three-dimensional method on a scientific basis by establishing average tissue thickness at certain identifiable regions over the face. Virchow (1905 ; 1914) suggested facial reconstruction on one side so as to provide a better relationship of the finished face to the underlying bony structures. Later McGregor (1915) and Wilder (1912 ;1918) modified the existing techniques by adding certain new dimensions regarding placement of eyes, ear, nose and mouth according to their dimensions. Krogman (1939) provided a list of tissue thickness at 13 identified points over the face. Snow et al. (1970) were the first to test likenesses objectively on several skulls using Krogman's method.

The Comparative method provides a high degree of accuracy when photographs and radiographs are involved in establishing identity. This may be achieved either through metric measurements or by superimposition technique. Of these techniques of identification, superimposition is more widely used and accepted (Chandra Sekharan, 1971 ; Narayan Reddy, 1973; and Rao et al., 1986). The evidential value of identification through superimposition technique in the court of law is, however, corroborative, certain rare characteristics may further help in arriving at a positive conclusion.

2. **Metric Measurements**

It is possible to assess whether the photograph of the skull could be of that individual whose identification photograph is available on the basis of certain anthropometric measurements on the photograph. With the help of these measurements, certain ratios can be calculated which exhibit least physical variation and hence render positive identification (Rao et al., 1984).

In order to accomplish this task following measurements are essential to be recorded on photographs:

a. Nasion—subnasale distance
b. Nasion—prosthion distance
c. Glabella—subnasale distance
d. Nasion—gnathion distance
e. Glabella—prosthion distance
f. Glabella—gnathion distance
g. Malar—malar distance
h. Zygion—zygion distance
i. Gonion—gonion distance
j. Alare—alarė distance

Different length-breadth ratios are calculated on the basis of these measurements for the purpose of comparison. If the difference between the ratios thus calculated is less than 0.06% it is taken to be similar and if the difference exceeds beyond this limit than the question of similarity does not arise. This method actually helps in deciding whether to proceed with the superimposition technique or not.

3. Superimposition Technique

The conventional technique of superimposition involves the preparation of negative plates of the photograph and the skull. Then these negatives are placed one over the other to procure a superimposed positive print. This is done to affirm whether the skull in question and the photograph belong to the same person or not and for this it is necessary to have a recent photograph of the person in front view with a slight lateral tilt.

In case the negative of the identification photograph is not available, it is prepared and placed under the ground glass of the camera and the facial outline and the specific landmarks are marked on the ground glass. The skull, in question, is then fixed on a tripod stand and placed n front of the camera. It is so positioned that it aligns with the facial outline marked on the ground glass as far as possible giving due allowance to the soft tissues covering the lines. A negative of the skull in this position is prepared and then the two negatives of the skull and identification photograph are superimposed taking all precautions that the following points on one are coinciding with that of other :

a. Nasion
b. Prosthion
c. Gnathion
d. Gonion
e. Zygion
f. Mid-sagittal plane
g. Horizontal line formed by joining the two supraorbital ridges.

After ascertaining the position of these landmarks the two superimposed negatives are photographed and a positive print is obtained, which brings out the similarities and dissimilarities between the skull and the photograph. The superimposition is said to be perfect only if the facial contour and the size of the skull correspond accurately after giving due allowance for the soft tissues.

The measurement of interpupillary distance on the life size skull photograph is another important factor because this distance is constant for the normal adults, (who do not exhibit any type of squint) as both the pupils, among them, move simultaneously so that their interpupillary distance remains constant. The mid-point of the orbit is determined by deciding both the orbits geometrically and then this distance is adjusted before enlargement of the questioned photograph for the purpose of superimposition.

From the forensic point of view the most informative examples of the application of this approach are provided by the head of a criminal executed in Egypt (Derry, 1934) ; the head of an embalmed cadaver from a medical institution in England (Glaister and Brash, 1937), and two skulls from the Ruxton murder case in England. Subsequent to getting a clear photograph of the Egyptian's head following execution, Derry was able to photograph the macerated skull in the same position and show that the skull fitted the face convincingly when the two views were superimposed. Brash followed the same technique with his cadaver head and with equally good results.

It may finally be stated that the comparison of a skull to portrait is in general a historic exercise, but a useful technique to emphasise the variability and individuality of such a procedure. The comparison of skull to photograph, on the other hand, is more useful and may help to establish identity. Using the superimposition technique to portraits or facial photographs and the skull tracings can help in restoring identity. While in order to reconstruct the face, the use of tissue thickness to model a head from skull is extremely useful. Eyes, nose, ear, and mouth can be reconstructed as part of a physiognomic restoration. But restoration of the skin colour can hardly be recreated. However, this adds much more to the individualisation of skeletal remains.

CHAPTER 11

EXPERT WITNESS AND TESTIMONY

During most trials where expert testimony is required regarding skeletal remains, a forensic anthropologist can expect to be called in the proceedings because the human skeletal remains involved usually signify a homicide. As such forensic anthropologists are important in establishing the *corpus delicti,* i.e. the body of the crime. The *corpus delicti* primarily constitutes the substantial and fundamental fact of the death of the person alleged to have been murdered, as a result of criminal agency. The *corpus delicti* can be any part of a skeleton that appears to the expert to be human and to confirm to the description of the suspected victim.

A prosecutor, before asking a forensic anthropologist to describe his results of the examination of skeletal remains, inquire when and from whom he received the remains and how the examination was done. Through these questions a prosecutor establishes the witness' part of the *chain of possession of the remains* and to connect this evidence with that of other witnesses, thereby providing confirmation that the court is dealing with remains of the assumed victim (Stewart, 1979).

Dwight (1878) was of the opinion that a witness must bear in mind the following directives.

Let the expert never forget that the result does not concern him while giving his evidence and making investigations.

He would not permit himself to be employed either to prove that the remains are those of a certain person, or that they are not.

He should be as impartial as a judge.

He should also remember that absolute certainty can very rarely be achieved in the solution of questions of this nature ; exceptions and various causes of error are so many that strong probability, amounting sometimes to moral certainty, is the most he can generally hope for.

Ultimately, it is the jury, not the expert, to decide on the identity of the skeleton, it is for the expert to show whether the identity is possible or probable.

The opinion he will give will depend not only on his professional acquirements, but on his honesty and common sense.

In connection with the expert witness, Philipps (1977) points out that once the cross-examination is over the prosecution has an opportunity on redirect examination to rehabilitate (the witness') trial credibility if by chance it has been impeached. Unless there is a full understanding by the prosecutor of not only what (the witness) did, but also why (the witness) followed a particular procedure, he will be unable to ask the necessary rehabilitation questions that will enable (the witness) to give answers which will restore (the witness') credibility.

Thus while giving testimony a forensic anthropologist should make every effort to maintain composure and to give the impression of being confident.

From time to time while testifying a forensic anthropologist will need to admit that an exact estimate of some traits cannot be given, e.g. age on the basis of molar-root ossification cannot be stated reliably within a certain range of probable error. This is an inherent limitation in human populations and should be frankly admitted even though it provides sufficient material for use to defence lawyer in his cross-examination.

In connection with cross-examination Philipps (1977) states that a forensic anthropologist may be shocked in confronting a defence lawyer not only versed in the skills of the courtroom, but also possessing substantial expertise in the scientific field about which the expert witness is testifying.

Such a proficiency on the part of the defence lawyers makes it necessary for a forensic anthropologist when serving as an expert witness to rely on more than subjective impressions in formulating opinions.

A witness must remain in the vicinity of the court until granted permission by the judge to leave.

BIBLIOGRAPHY

1. ALLBROOK, D. 1961.
   The Estimation of Stature in British and East African Males. Based on Tibial and Ulnar Bone Lengths. *J. For. Med.*, 8 : 15-28.
2. ATHWALE, M.C. 1963.
   Estimation of Height from Lengths of Forearm Bones : A Study of One Hundred Maharashtran Male Adults of Ages between 25 and 30 years. *Am. J. Phys. Anthropol.*, 21 : 105-112.
3. BADKUR, P. 1985.
   Estimation of Bone Length and Stature from Measurements of Human Long Bones of Madhya Pradesh, India. Ph. D. Thesis, University of Delhi.
4. BASS, W.M. 1971.
   Human Osteology : A Laboratory anḍ Field Mannual of Human Skeleton. Columbia, Missouri Archaeological Society.
5. BASS, W.M. 1979.
   Developments in the Identification of Human Skeletal Material (1968-1978). *Am. J. Phys. Anthropol.*, 51 : 555-562.
6. BLACK, T.K. 1978.
   A New Method for Assessing Sex of Fragmentary Skeletal Remain : Femoral Shaft Circumference. *Am. J. Phys. Anthropol.*, 48 : 227-231.

7. BOULINIER, G. 1968.
La Determination du Sexe des Cranes Humaines a I'aide des Fonctions Discriminantes. *Bull. Mem. Soc. d'Anthropol. Paris. 12th Series.* 3 : 301-316

8. BOULINIER, G. 1969.
Variations avec I'age du Dimorphisme Sexuel des Cranes Humains Adulte. Influence sur les Possibilities de Discrimination Statistique des Sujects. *Bull. Mem. Soc. d'Anthropol. Paris. 12th Series.* 4 : 127-138.

9. BREITINGER, E. 1937.
Zur Berechnung der Korperhohe aus den Langen Gleidmassenknochen. *Anthrop. Anz.*, 14 : 249-274.

10. BROCA, P. 1876.
Sur la Trepanation du Crane et les Amulettes Cranienne a L'epoque Neolitique. Paris, Ernest Leroux.

11. BROOKS, S.T. 1955.
Skeletal Age at Death : The Reliability of Cranial and Pubic Age Indicators. *Am. J. Phys. Anthropol.*, 13 : 567-597.

12. BROTHWELL, D.R. 1965.
Digging up Bones. London, The British Museum of Natural History.

13. BRUES, A.M. 1958.
Identification of Skeletal Remains. *J. Crim. Law, Criminol. and Police Sci.*, 48 : 551-653.

14. BRUNO, G. 1934.
Uber Senile Strukturveranderungen der Proximalen Humerusepiphyse. *Fortschr Roentgenstr*, 50 : 287-289.

15. CHANDRA SEKHARAN, P. 1971.
A Revised Superimposition Technique for Identification of the Individual from the Skull and Photographs. *J. Crim. Law, Criminol. and Police Sci.* 69 : 107 : 113.

16. CHAURASIA, B.D. 1983.
Handbook of General Anatomy. Delhi, CBS.

17. CHAURASIA, B.D. 1984.
Human Osteology. Delhi, CBS.

18. COOK, S.F. and HEIZER, R.F. 1947.
The Quantitative Investigation of Aboriginal Sites :

Analyses of Human Bones. *Am. J. Phys. Anthropol.*, 5 : 201-219.

19. CORNWALL, I.W. 1956.
Bones for the Archaeologist. New York, Macmillan.
20. DAHLBERG. A.A. 1950.
The Evolutionary Significance of the Protostylid, *Am. J. Phys. Anthropol.*, 8 : 15-27.
21. DERRY, D.E. 1934.
Cited by Stewart, T.D. 1979.
22. DORSE, G.A. 1897.
A Sexual Study of the Size of the Articular Surfaces of the long Bones in Aboriginal American Skeletons. *Boston Med. Surg. J.*, 137 : 80-82.
23. DUGGAL, N. and NATH, S. 1986.
Estimation of Stature using Percutaneous Lengths of Radius, Ulna, and Tibia Among Lodhas and Mundas of District Midnapore, West Bengal. *Anthropologie*, 24 : 24-30.
24. DUPERTUIS, C.W. and HADDEN, J.A. 1951.
On the Reconstruction of Stature from Long Bones. *Am. J. Phys. Anthropol.*, 9 : 15-53.
25. DWIGHT, T. 1878.
The Identification of the Human Skeleton : A Medico-Legal Study. Boston, Massachusetts Medical Society.
26. DWIGHT, T. 1881.
The Sternum as an Index of Sex and Age. *J. Anat. Physiol. London*. 15 : 327-330.
27. DWIGHT, T. 1884.
Methods of Estimating the Height from the parts of the Skeleton. *Med. Rec. N.Y.* 46 : 293-296.
28. DWIGHT, T. 1890.
The sternum as an Index of Sex, Height and Age. *J. Anat. Physiol. London*. 24 : 527-535
29. DWIGHT, T. 1905.
The Size of the Articular Surfaces of the Long Bones as Characteristics of Sex : An Anthropological Study. *Am. J. Anat.*, 4 : 19-32.
30. EL-NAJJAR, M.Y. and McWILLIAMS, K.R. 1978.
Forensic Anthropology, Springfield, Thomas.

31. FISHER, A., KHUM, G. and ADAMI, G. 1931.
Dental Pathology of the Prehistoric Indians of Wisconsin. *Bulletin of the Public Museum of the City of Milwaukee.*

32. FREDERIC, J. 1906.
Untersuchungen uber die Normale Obliteration der Schadelnahte. *Z. Morph. Anthropol.*, 9 : 373-456.

33. FUJII, A. 1958.
On the Relation of Long Bone Lengths of Limbs to Stature. *Juntendo Daigaku Taiiku Gakubu Kiyo (Jutendo Univ. Bull. Phys. Ed.)*, 3 : 49-61.

34. FULLY, G. 1956.
Une Nouvelle Methode de Determination de la Taille. *Ann. Med. Leg., Criminol.*, 36 : 266-273.

35. GARN. S.M. 1972.
The Course of Bone Gain and Phases of Bone Loss. *Orthopedic Clinics of North America.* 3 : 503-526.

36. GILBERT, B.M. 1973.
Mammalian Osteo-Archaeology : North America. Columbia, Missouri Archaeological Society.

37. GILBERT, B.M. and McKERN, T.W. 1973.
A Method for Aging the Female os Pubis. *Am. J. Phys. Anthropol.*, 38 : 31-38.

38. GILES, E. 1964.
Sex Determination by Discriminant Function Analysis of the Mandible. *Am. J. Phys. Anthropol.*, 22 : 129-135.

39. GILES, E. 1970.
Discriminant Function Sexing of the Human Skeleton. In Stewart, T.D. (Ed) : *Personal Identification in Mass Disasters.* pp 99-109. Washington, National Museum of Nature History.

40. GILES, E. and ELLIOT, O. 1960.
Negro-White Identification from the Skull. *Proc. 6th Internat. Anth. Cong.*, Paris (Unpublished).

41. GILES, E. and ELLIOT, O. 1963.
Sex Determination by Discriminant Function Analysis of Crania. *Am. J. Phys. Anthropol.*, 21 : 53-58.

42. GLAISTER, J. and BRASH, J.C. 1937.

Medico-Legal Aspects of Ruxton Case. Edinburgh, E. & S. Livingstone.

43. GOLDMAN, A.D. 1982.
"The Scope of Forensic Dentistry" in *Outline of Forensic Dentistry* (eds.) J.A. Cottone and S.M. Standish Chicago. Year-book Medical Publishers Inc.,
44. GRAVES, W.W. 1922.
Observations on Age-Changes in the Scapula. A Preliminary Note. *Am. J. Phys. Anthropol.,* 5 : 21.
45. GREULICH, W.W. and PYLE, S.I. 1959.
Radiographic Atlas of Skeletal Development of the Hand and Wrist. California. Stanford University Press, Stanford.
46. GURDJIAN, E.S. WEBSTER, J.E. and LISSNER, H.R. 1950.
The Mechanism of Skull Fracture. *Radiol.,* 54 : 313-339.
47. GUSTAFSON, G. 1950.
Age Determination on Teeth. *J. Am. Dent. Assn.* 41 : 45-54.
48. GUSTAFSON, G. 1966.
Forensic Odontology. New York. American Elsevier.
49. HANIHARA, K. 1958.
Sexual Diagnosis of Japanese Long Bones by Means of Discriminant Function. *J. Anthrop. Soc. Nippon,* 66 : 187-196.
50. HANIHARA, K. 1959.
Sex Diagnosis of Japanese Skulls and Scapulae by Means of Discriminant Function. *J. Anthrop. Soc. Nippon,* 67 : 191-197.
51. HASEN, G. 1954.
Die Altersbestimmung am Proximalen Humerus und Femurende in Rahmen der Identifizierung Menschlicher Skelettreste. *Wiss Z. Humboldt Universitat Berlin.* Math : naturwiss. Reihe 3 : 1-73.
52. HELFMAN, P.M. and BADA, J.L. 1976.
Aspartic Acid Racemisation in Dentine as a Measure of Aging. *Nature,* 262 : 279-281.
53. HIS, W. 1895.
Anatomische Forschungen ueber Johann Sebastian Bach's

Gebeine und Antlitz' nebst Bemerkungen ueber dessen Bilder. *Abhandl d k Sachs Gesellsch d Wissensch Zu Leipz.* 22 : 379-420.

54. HOTTON, E.A. 1943.
Medico-Legal Aspects of Physical Anthropology. *Clinics,* 1 : 1612-1624.

55. HOSIMOTA, M. 1938.
Ethnologishe Untersuchungen ueber die Unterextremitacts—Knocher der Chinesen. *J. Orient. Med.* 29 : 32-34.

56. HRDLICKA, A. 1932.
The Principal Dimensions, Absolute and Relative, of the Humerus in the White Race. *Am. J. Phys. Anthropol.*, 16: 431-450.

57. HRDLICKA, A. 1942.
The Adult Scapula ; Additional Observations and Measurements. *Am. J. Phys. Anthropol.*, 29 : 363-415.

58. HYRTL, J. 1865.
Handbuch der Topographischen Anatomie, etc. 2 vol. Wein.

59. IGNALLS, N.W. 1924.
Studies on the Femur. *Am. J. Phys. Anthropol.*, 7 : 207-255.

60. JIT, I. and SINGH, S. 1966.
The Sexing of the Adult Clavicles. *Ind. J. Med. Res.*, 54 : 1-21.

61. JOHNSTON, F.E. 1962,
Growth of the Long Bones of Infants and Young Children at Indian knoll. *Am. J. Phys. Anthropol.*, 20 : 249-254.

62. JONES, F. WOOD, 1930-31.
The Non-Metric Morphological Characters of the Skull as Criteria for Racial Diagnosis. *J. Anat.* 65 : 368-378.

63. JOSHI, N.B., PATEL, M.P. and DONGRE, A.V. 1964.
Regression Equation of Height on Ulnar Length. *Ind. J. Med. Res.*, 52 : 1087-1091.

64. KARUS, B.S. 1959.
Occurrence of the Carabelli Trait in Southwest Ethnic Groups. *Am. J. Phys. Anthrop.*, 17 : 117-123.

65. KATE, B.R., 1964.

A Study of the Regional Variation of the Indian Femur : The Diameter of the Head, its Medicolegal and Surgical Applications. *J. Anat. Soc. India*, 13 : 80-84.

66. KATE, B.R. and MAJUMDAR, R.D. 1976.
Stature Estimation from Femur and Humerus by Regression and Autometry. *Acta Anat.*, 94 : 311-320.

67. KERLEY, E.R. 1965.
The Microscopic Determination of Age in Human Bone. *Am. J. Phys. Anthropol.*, 23 : 149-163.

68. KERLEY, E.R. 1973.
Forensic Anthropology. In Weath, C.H. (Ed.) *Legal Medicine Annual* 1973. pp. 161-198 New York, Appleton-Century-Crofts.

69. KHAN, E.N. 1959.
In "Modi's Textbook of Medical Jurisprudence and Toxicology". 13th ed., Bombay, M.N. Tripathi.

70. KINZELY, I. 1973.
On the Possibilities and Methods of the Chemical Determination of Sex from Bones. *OSSA*, 1 : 51-62.

71. KOLLMANM, J. 1898.
Die Weichteile des Gesichts und die Persistenz der Rassen. *Anat. Anz.*, 15 : 165-177.

72. KOLTE, P.M. and BANSAL, P.C. 1974.
Determination of Regression Formula for Reconstruction of Stature from Long Bones of Upper Limb in Maharashtrians of Marathwada Region. *J. Anat. Soc. India*, 23 : 6-11.

73. KROGMAN, W.M. 1939.
A Guide to the Identification of Human Skeletal Material. *FBI Law Enf. Bull.* 8 : 3-31.

74. KROGMAN, W.M. 1949.
The Human Skeleton in Legal Medicine : Medical Aspects. In Levinson, S.D. (Ed.) *Symposium on Medico-legal Problems* Ser. 2, pp. 1-90. Philadelphia, Lippincott.

75. KROGMAN, W.M. 1955.
The Skeleton in Forensic Medicine. *Grad. Med.*, (2 & 3) Feb.-March.

76. KROGMAN, W.M. 1962.

The Human Skeleton in Forensic Medicine. Springfield, Thomas.

77. LECLERCQ, M. 1969.
Entomological Parasitology—The Relations between Entomology and the Medical Sciences. New York, Pergamon.

78. LEWIS, A.B. and GARN, S.M. 1960.
The Relationship between Tooth Formation and other Maturational Factors. *Angle Orthodont.*, 30 : 70-77.

79. LORKE, D., MUNZNER, H. and WALTER, E. 1953.
Zur Rekonstruktion der Korpergrosse eines Menschen aus den Langen Gliedmassenknocken. *Deutsch Z. Ger. Gerichtl. Med.*, 42 : 189-202.

80. MACDONNEL, W.R. 1901.
On Criminal Anthropometry and the Identification of Criminals. *Biometrika,* 1 : 177-227.

81. MANOUVRIER, L. 1892.
Determination de la Taille de'apres les Grands os des Members. *Rev. Mem. de l'Ecole d'Anth.*, 2: 227-233.

82. MANT, A.K. and FURBANK, R. 1957.
Adipocere-A Review. *J. For. Med.*, 4 : 18-35.

83. McKERN, T.W. and STEWART, T.D. 1957.
Skeletal Age Changes in Young American Males. Analysed from the Standpoint of Age Identification. *Environmental Protection Res. Div. Tech. Rep. EP-45.*

84. MENDES-CORREA, A.A. 1932.
La Taille de Portugais d'apres les os Longes. *Anthropologie, Prague,* 10 : 268-272.

85. MODI, J.P. 1977.
Medical Jurisprudence and Toxicology. Bombay, Tripathi Pvt. Ltd.

86. MULLER, G. 1935.
Zur Bestimmung der Lange Beschadigter Extermitatenknochen. *Anthrop. Anz.*, 12 : 70-72.

87. NARAYAN REDDY, K.S. 1973.
Identification of Dismembered Parts : The Medico-legal Aspects of the Nagaraju Case. *Forensic Science,* 2 : 351-374.

88. NAT, B.S. 1931.
Estimation of Stature from Long Bones of the United

Provinces : A Medico-legal Inquiry in Anthropometry. *Ind. J. Med. Res.*, 18 : 1245-1253.

89. NATH. S. 1987.
Forensic Anthropology : A New Dimension to the Study of Skeletal Material. *Spectra of Anthropological Progress.* 9 : 35-40.

90. NATH, S. 1988.
Formulation of Linear Regression Equations for Prediction of Stature through Percutaneous Lengths of Radius, Ulna and Tibia Among Lodha Males. (Unpublished).

91. NATH, S. 1988.
Multiple Regression Equations for Estimation of Stature using Percutaneous Lengths of the Baigas and the Gonds of Madhya Pradesh. (Unpublished).

92. NATH, S. and SATISH CHANDRA, N. 1986.
Computation of New Multiplication Factors for Stature Estimation from Percutaneous Lengths of Radius and Tibia. *Police Research and Development Journal.* Qr. I : 13-15.

93. NATH, S., DUGGAL, N. and SATISH CHANDRA, N. 1987.
Stature Estimation through Percutaneous Lengths of Ulna and Tibia Among Lodhas of District Midnapore, West Bengal. *Indian Journal of Forensic Sciences.* 1 : 67-74.

94. OLIVER, G. 1969.
Practical Anthropology. Springfield, Thomas.

95. OLIVER, G. and PINEAU, H. 1958.
Determination de l'age du Foetus et de L'embryon. *Arch. Anat.* 6 : 21-28.

96. ORFILA, M.J.B. 1821.
Lecons de Medecine Legale. Paris.

97. ORTNER, D.J., VONENDT, DAVID W. and ROBINSON, M.S. 1972.
The Effect of Temperature on Protein Decay in Bones. Its Significance in Nitrogen Dating of Archaeological Specimens. *Am. Antiq.*, 37 : 514-520.

98. PAN, N. 1924.

Length of Long Bones and their Proportion to Body Height in Hindus. *J. Anat.*, 58 : 3,4-378.

99. PATEL, M.P., JOSHI, N.B. and DONGRE, A.V. 1964.
Regression Equation of Height on Tibial Length. *Ind. J. Med. Res.*, 52 : 531-534.

100. PRARSON, K. 1917-19.
A Study of the Long Bones of the English Skeleton. I. The Femur. In Draper's Co. *Research Memoir*. University of London. Biometric Series X.

101. PHILIPPS, K.A. 1977.
The "Nuts and Bolts" of Testifying as a Forensic Scientist. *J. For. Sci.*, 22 : 457-463.

102. PICK, J.W., STACK, J.K. and ANSON, B.J. 1941.
Measurements on the Human Femur. I. Lengths, Diameters and Angles. *Quart. Bull. North W. Univ. Med. Sch.*, 15 : 281-290.

103. POMMERAL, F. 1869.
Recherche sur la Synostose des os du crane Consideree an Point de Vue Normal et Pathologique Chez les Differentes Races Humaines. These, Paris.

104. RAO, K.V.S., GUPTA, G.D. and SEHGAL, V.N. 1984.
Identification of a Person by Metric Measurements of Photographs. *Police Research & Development Journal.* Qr. III : 15-17.

105. RAO, K.V.S., GUPTA, G.D. and SEHGAL, V.N. 1986.
Identification of a Person by Superimposition Technique: A case Report. *Spectra of Anthropological Progress.* 8 : 37-42.

106. REID, R.W. 1927.
Remains of St. Magnus and St. Rognvald entomed in Saint Magnus Cathedral, Kirkwall, Orkney. *Biometrika*, 18 : 118-150.

107. RIBBE, F.C. 1885.
Etude sur L'ordre d' Obliteration des Sutures du Crane dans les Races Humaines. These, Paris.

108. ROMERO, J. 1958.
Mutilaciones Dentaires Prehispanicas deMexicoy America en General. Mexico, Instituto Nacional de Antropologia e Historia.

109. SIDDIQUI, M.A.M. 1934.
Variations in the Lower end of the Femur from Indians. *J. Anat.* 68 : 331-337.

110. SIDDIQUI, M.A.H. and SHAH, M.A. 1944.
Estimation of Stature from Long Bones of Punjabis. *Ind. J. Med. Res.*, 32 : 105-108.

111. SINGH, B. and SOHAL, H.S. 1952.
Estimation of Stature from the Length of Clavicle in Punjabees : A Preliminary Report. *Ind. J. Med. Res.*, 40 : 67-71.

112. SINGH, S. and SINGH, S.P. 1972.
Identification of Sex from Humerus. *Ind. J. Med. Res.*, 60 : 1061-1066.

113. SINGH, S. and SINGH, S.P. 1974.
Weight of the Femur ; A Useful Measurement for identification of Sex. *Acta. Anat.*, 87 : 141-145.

114. SINGH, S.P. and SINGH, S. 1973.
A Study of the Femoral Curvature Index in Indian Subjects. *J. Anat. Soc. India*, 22 : 86-89.

115. SCHOUR, I. and MASSLER, M. 1940.
Chart Entitled "Development of the Human Dentition" 2nd ed. Chicago, American Dental Association.

116. SCHRANZ, D. 1959.
Age Determination from the Internal Structure of the Humerus. *Am. J. Phys. Anthropol.*, 17 : 273-277.

117. SMITH, S. 1939.
Studies in Identification, No. 3 & No. 4. *Police J. London*, 12 : 274-285, 403-408.

118. SNOW. C.E. 1948.
Indentification of the Unknown War Dead. *Am. J. Phys. Anthropol.*, 6 : 323-328.

119. SNOW, C.C., GATLIFF, B.P. and McWILLIAMS, K.R. 1970.
Reconstruction of Facial Features From the Skull : An Evaluation of its Usefulness in Forensic Anthropology. *Am. J. Phys. Anthrop.*, 33 : 221-227.

120. STAHL, C.J. 1980.
Identification of Human Remains. In Spitz, W.U. and

Fisher, R.S. (Eds.). *Medico-Legal Aspects of Death.* pp. 39-70. Springfield, Thomas.

121. STANDISH, S.M. and STIMSON, P.G. 1977.
The Scope of Forensic Dentistry. *Dent. Clin. N. Amer.*, 21 : 3.

122. STEELE, D.G. and McKERN, T.M. 1969.
A Method for Assessment of Maximum Long Bone Length and Living Stature from Fragmentary Long Bones. *Am. J. Phys. Anthropol.*, 31 : 215-227.

123. STEVENSON, P.H. 1929.
On Racial Differences in Stature Long Bone Regression Formulae for the Chinese. *Biometrika*, 21 : 303-318.

124. STEWART, T.D. 1948.
Medico-legal Aspects of the Skeleton. 1. Sex, Age, Race and Stature. *Am. J. Phys. Anthropol.*, 6 : 315-322.

125. STEWART, T.D. 1968.
Identification by Skeletal Structures. In Camps, Francis E. (Ed) *Gradwohl's Legal Medicine*, 2nd ed. pp. 123-154. Bristol, Wright.

126. STEWART, T.D. 1973.
Recent Improvements in Estimating Stature, Sex, Age and Race from Skeletal Remains. In Mant A. Keith, (Ed.). *Modern Trends in Forensic Medicine*—3 pp. 193-211, London, Butterworths.

127. STEWART, T.D., 1979.
Essentials of Forensic Anthropology. Springfield, Illinois, Thomas.

128. SUE, J.J. 1955.
Sur les Proportions du Squelette de Homme, Examine Depuis L'age le Plus Tendre Jusqu'a Celui de Vingtcing, Soixante ans and au dela. *Mem. Math. et Phys. Acad. Sci. Paris*, 2 : 572-585.

129. TELKKA, A, 1950.
On the Prediction of Human Stature from the Long Bones. *Acta. Anat.*, 9 : 103-117.

130. TERRY, R.J. 1942.
Osteology and Articulations. In Schaeffer, J.P. (Ed.). *Morris' Human Anatomy* 10th ed. Sections III & IV. Philadelphia and Blackiston.

131. THIEME, F.P. 1957.
Sex in Negro Skeleton. *J. Forensic Med.*, 4 : 72-81.

132. THIEME, F. and SCHULL, W.J. 1957.
Sex Determination from the Skeleton. *Human Biol.* 29 : 242-273,

133. THOMSON, A. 1899.
The Sexual Differences of the Foetal Pelvis. *J. Anat. and Physiol. London.* 33 : 359-380.

134. TODD, T.W. 1920-21.
Age Changes in Pubic bone. *Am. J. Phys. Anthropol.*, 3 : 285-334. 4 : 1-70, 333-424,

135. TODD, T.W. and LYON, D.W. Jr. 1924-25.
Cranial Suture Closure : Its Progress and Age Relationship-I & II. *Am. J. Phys. Anthropol.*, 7 : 325-384, 8 : 23-71 ; 149-168.

136. TOPINARD, P. 1888.
La Formule de Reconstitution de la Taille d' apres les os Longs. *Rev. Anthropol.*, 3 : 469-471.

137. TROTTER, M. 1970.
Estimation of Stature from Intact Long Limb Bones. In Stewart, T.D. (Ed.) : *Personal Identification in Mass Disasters.* pp. 71-83. Washington, National Museum of Natural History.

138. TROTTER, M. and GLESER, G.C. 1952.
Estimation of Stature from Long Bones of American Whites and Negroes. *Am. J. Phys. Anthropol.*, 10 : 463-514,

139. TROTTER, M. and GLESER, G.C. 1958.
A Re-evaluation of Stature based on Measurements taken during Life and of Long Bones after Death. *Am. J. Phys. Anthropol.*, 16 : 79-123.

140. TROTTER, M. and PETERSON, R.R. 1955.
Ash Weight of Human Skeletons in Percent of their Dry. Fat-free Weight. *Anat. Rec.*, 123 : 341-368.

141. UBELAKER, D.H., PHENICE, and BASS, W.M. 1969.
Artificial Interproximal Grooving of the Teeth in American Indians. *Am. J. Phys. Anthropol.*, 30 : 145-149.

142. VIRCHOW, H. 1905.

Einen kofp, der zur Halfe aus dem Schadel zur Halfe aus der Gesichtsmaske Bestcht. *Z. Ethnol.*, 37 : 781-783.

143. VIRCHOW, H. 1912.
Die Anthropologische Untersuchung der Nase. *Z. Ethnol.*, 44 : 289-327.

144. WALHOLZ, L. 1894.
Uber die Altersbestimmung an Leichen auf Grund des Ossifikation-sprozesses im obern Humerusende. *Friedreich's Bl Gerichtl Med. Nurnb.*, 45 : 210-219.

145. WALMSLEY, T. 1933.
A Vertical Axes of the Femur and their Relations. *J. Anat.*, 67 : 284-300.

146. WELCKER, H. 1883.
Schiller's Schadel and Todenmaske nebst Mittheilungen Uber Schadel und Todenmaske Kants, Braunschweig.

147. WELLS, C. 1959.
A Study of Cremation. *Antiquity*, 34 : 29-37.

148. WILDER, H.H. 1912.
The Physiognomy of the Indians of Southern New England. *Am. Anthropol.*, 14 : 415-436.

149. WILDER, H.H. and WENTWORTH, B. 1918.
Personal Identification : Methods for the Identification of Individuals, Living or Dead. Boston, Gorham.

150. WILLIAMS, A.C. 1976.
Unexpected Death due to Natural Disease. In Camps F.E. (Ed.). *Grahdwohl's Legal Medicine*, 3rd ed. pp. 220-225. Bristol, Wright.